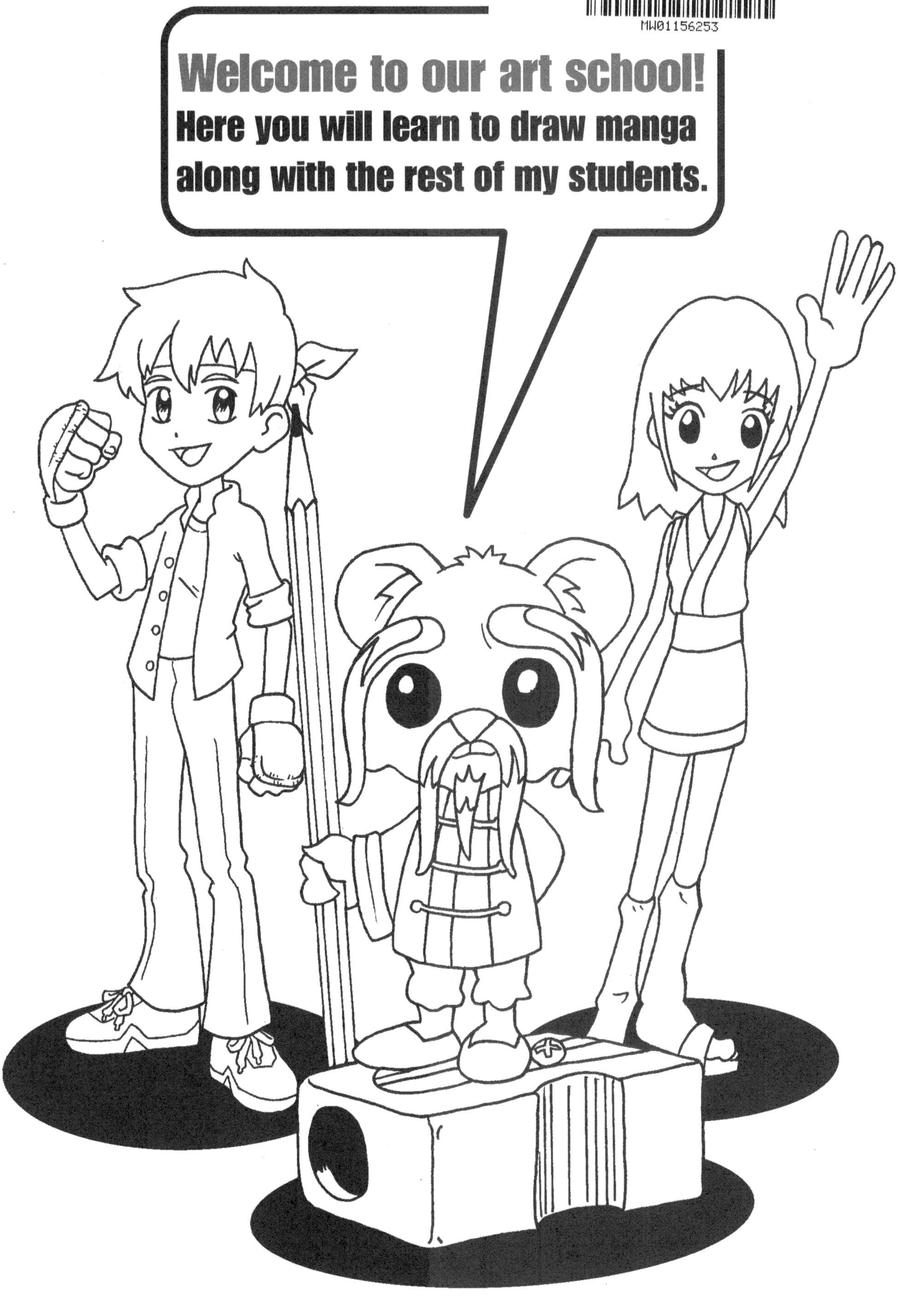
Welcome to our art school!
Here you will learn to draw manga along with the rest of my students.

MW01156253

CHAPTER 1
Basic Techniques

How to Draw
MANGA

Andrés Bernardo Giannotta

Dover Publications, Inc.
Mineola, New York

Bibliographical Note

How to Draw Manga is a new work, first published by
Dover Publications, Inc., in 2010.

International Standard Book Number

ISBN-13: 978-0-486-47662-9
ISBN-10: 0-486-47662-6

Manufactured in the United States by LSC Communications
47662606   2017
www.doverpublications.com

MATERIALS

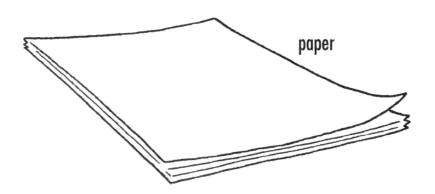

paper

These are the things that
you will need to learn
to draw manga.

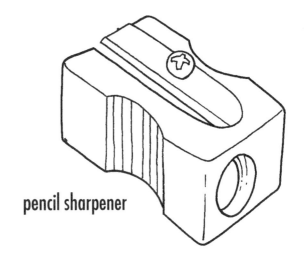

pencil sharpener

pencils

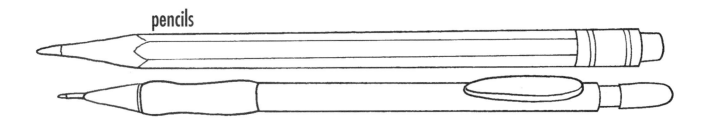

MATERIALS

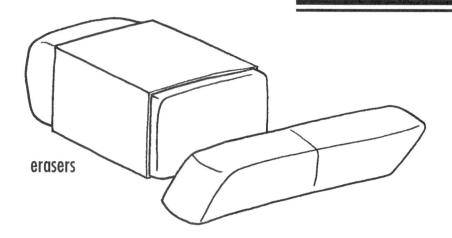

erasers

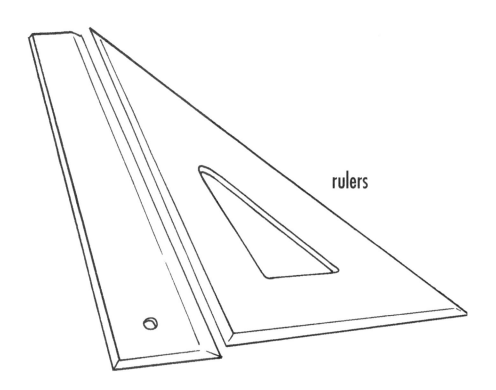

rulers

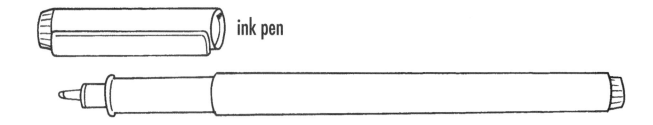

ink pen

BASIC SHAPES

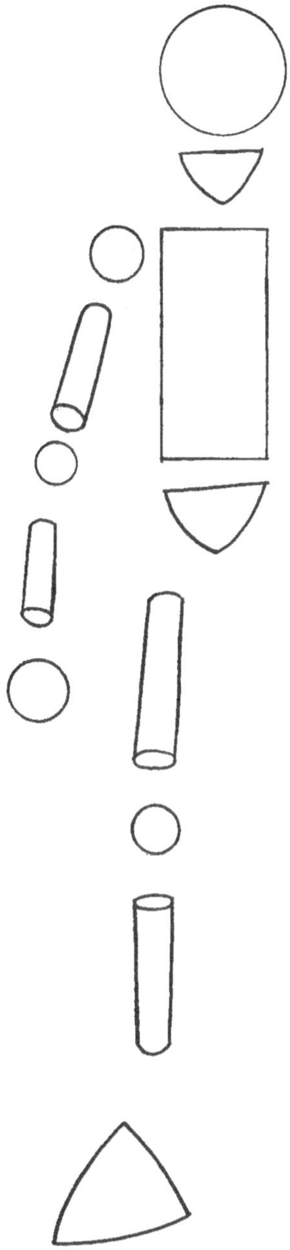

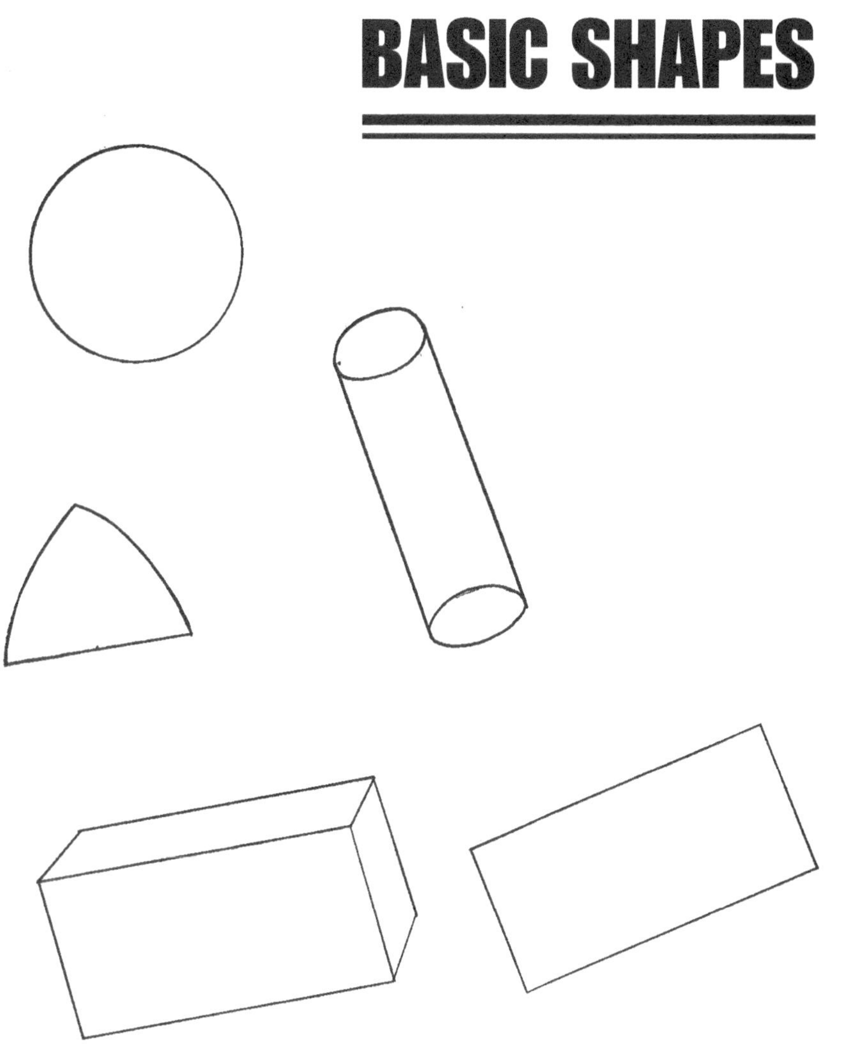

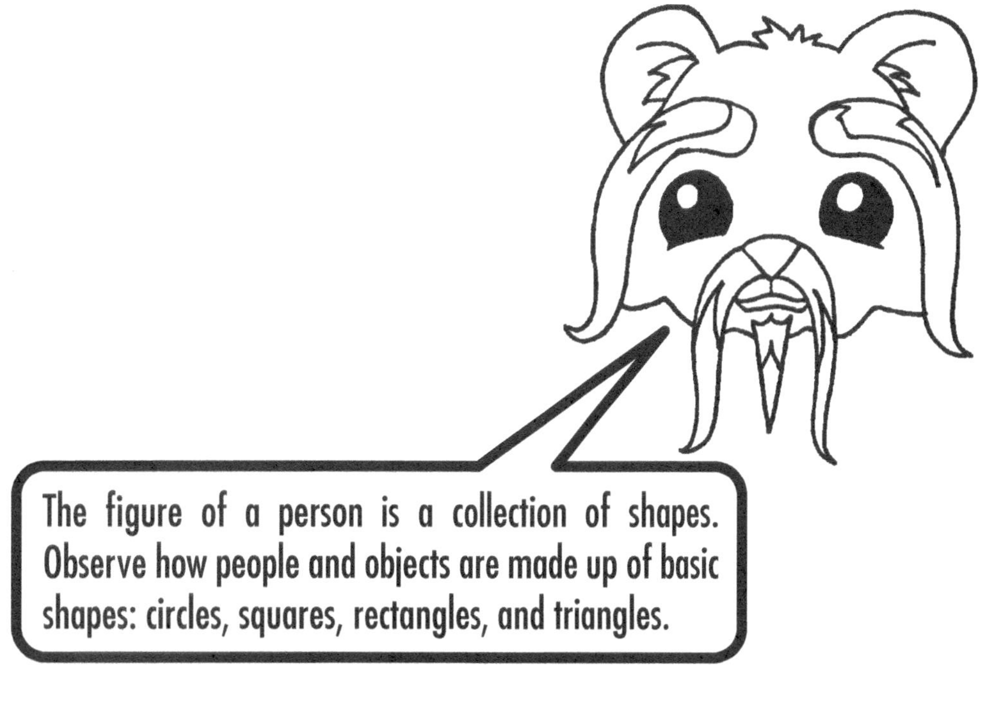

The figure of a person is a collection of shapes. Observe how people and objects are made up of basic shapes: circles, squares, rectangles, and triangles.

THE FACE

How to draw the head

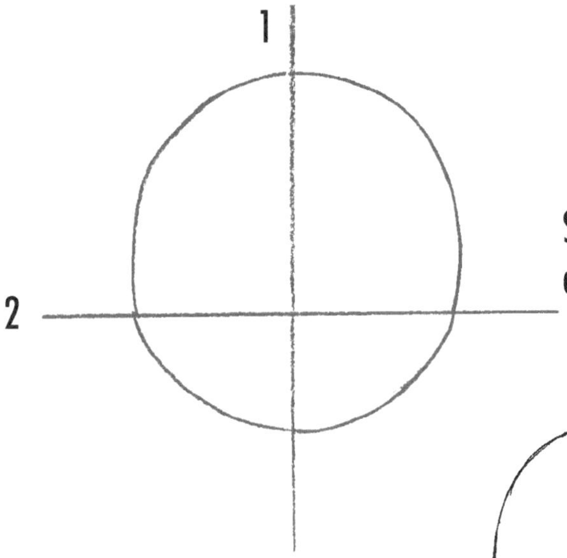

Step 1: Draw a circle. Draw a vertical line [1] and a horizontal line [2] over it.

Step 2: Draw the chin. Over line [2], draw the eyes. The distance between them should be approximately the width of one eye.

Step 3: The nose is drawn over the vertical line. The ears begin at the nose's height and end at the eyes' height, as shown.

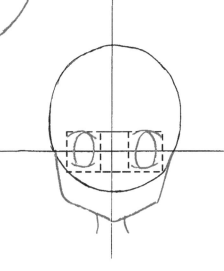

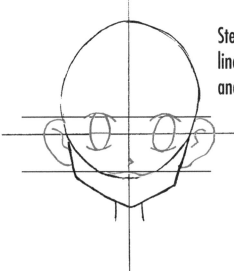

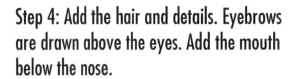

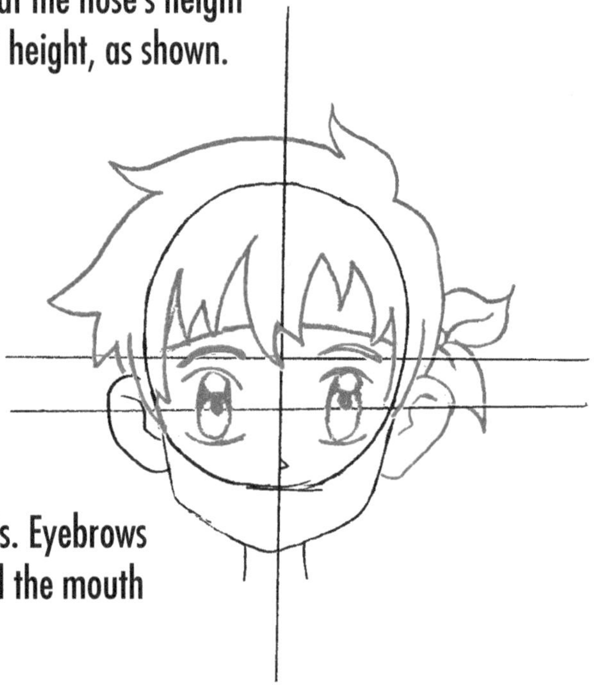

Step 4: Add the hair and details. Eyebrows are drawn above the eyes. Add the mouth below the nose.

FACIAL EXPRESSIONS

Learning to draw facial expressions allows us to show the characters' emotions. This helps us tell a better story.

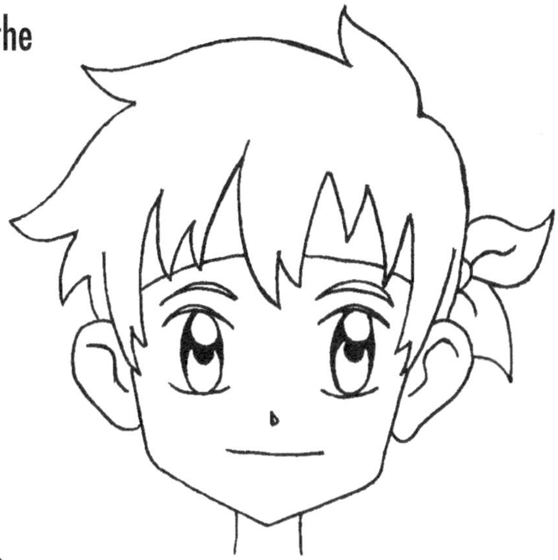

Standard

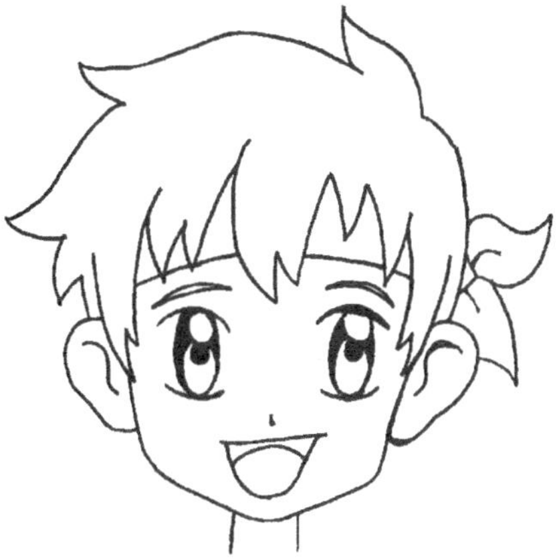

Happy

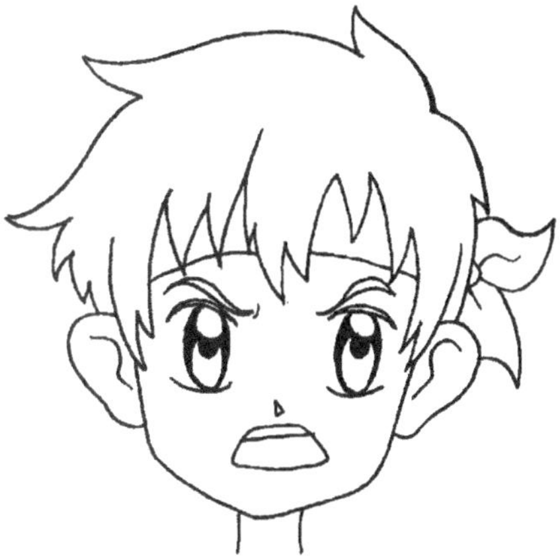

Angry

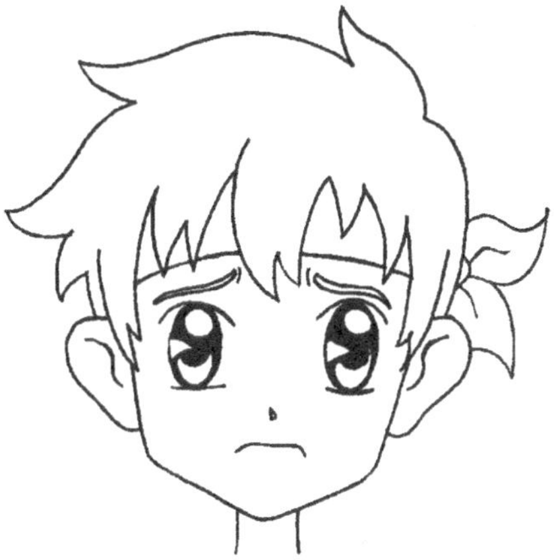

Sad

You can create facial expressions by modifying the eyebrows, eyes, and mouth.

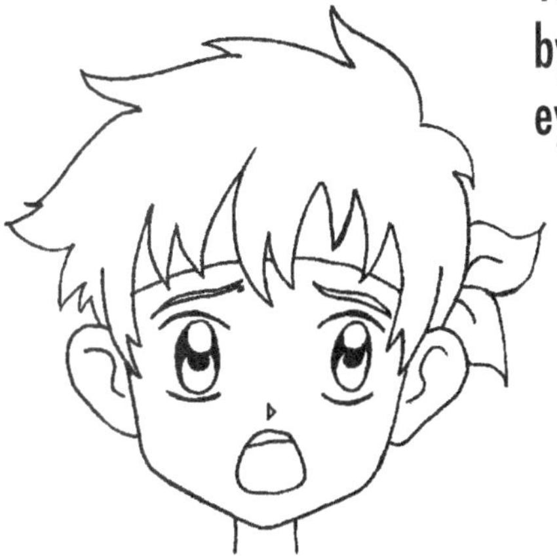

Scared

THE BODY

A ten-year-old manga character is approximately "four heads" tall.

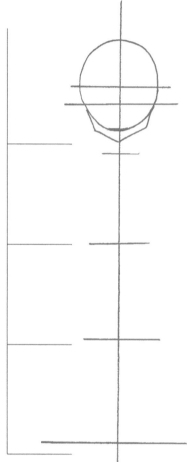

Step 1: Trace a vertical line and divide it into four equal parts. Draw the character's head in the first part.

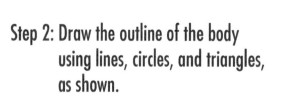

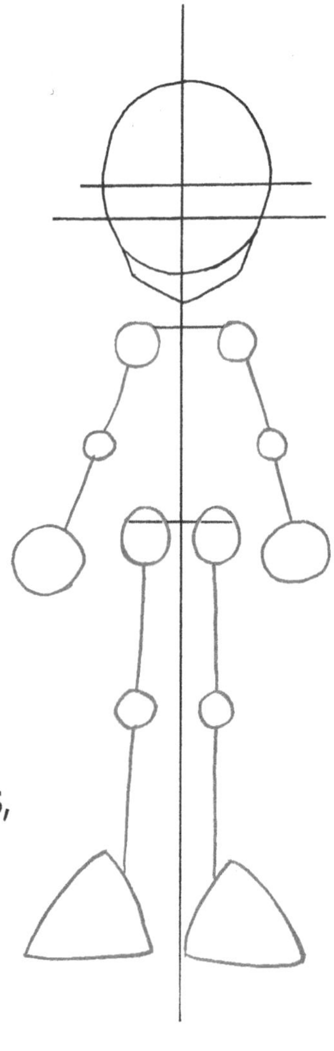

Step 2: Draw the outline of the body using lines, circles, and triangles, as shown.

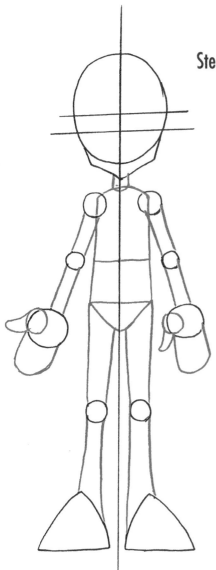

Step 3: Add volume to your character's body.
Draw a structure for the fingers.

Tips

- Shoulders start between the first and second "head."
- The elbows begin at the halfway point of the second head.
- The hips start between the second and third heads. The hands do too.
- The knees begin at the third head.

The number of "heads" you use depends on the character's structure.

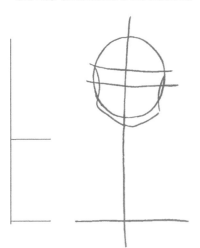

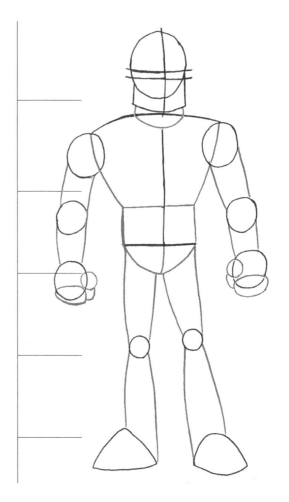

MOVEMENT

Use guidelines like this one to show movement.

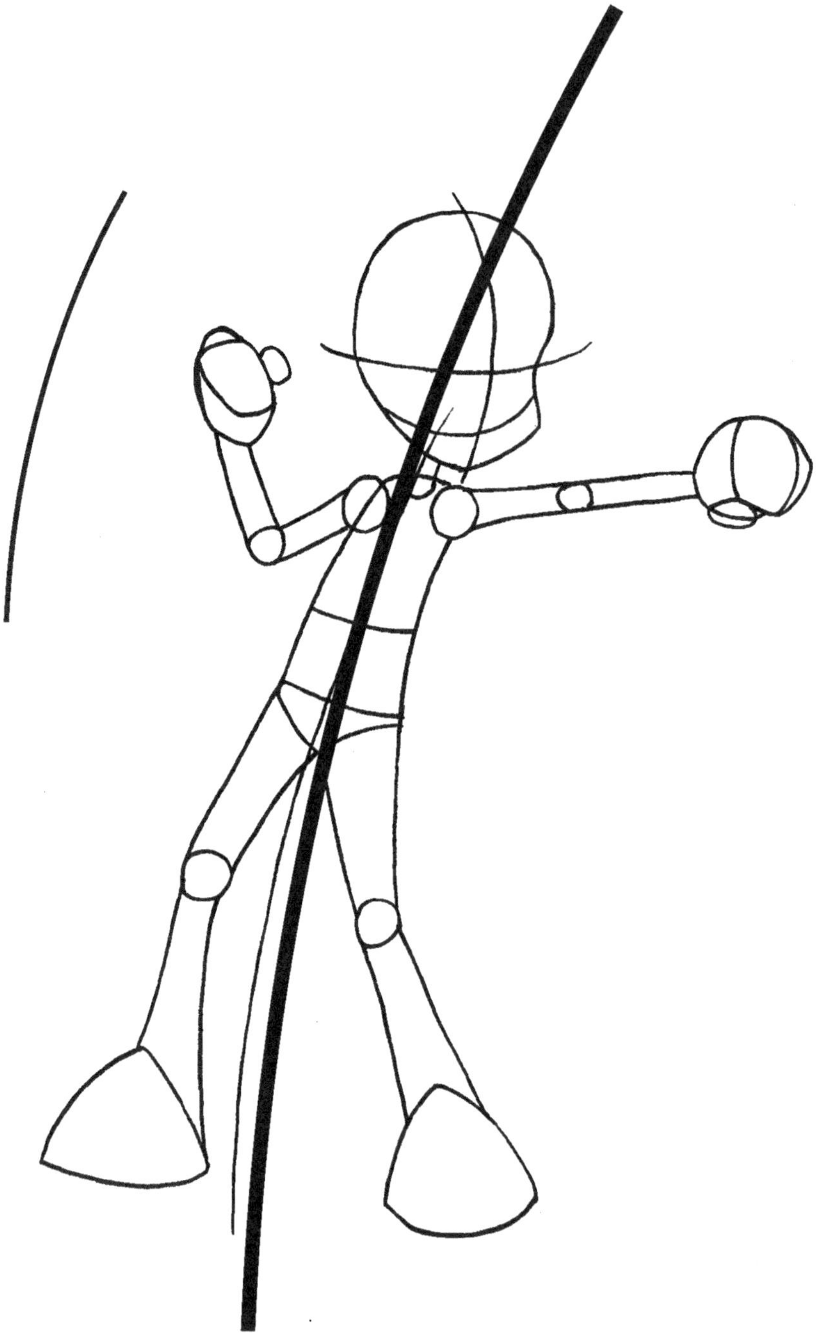

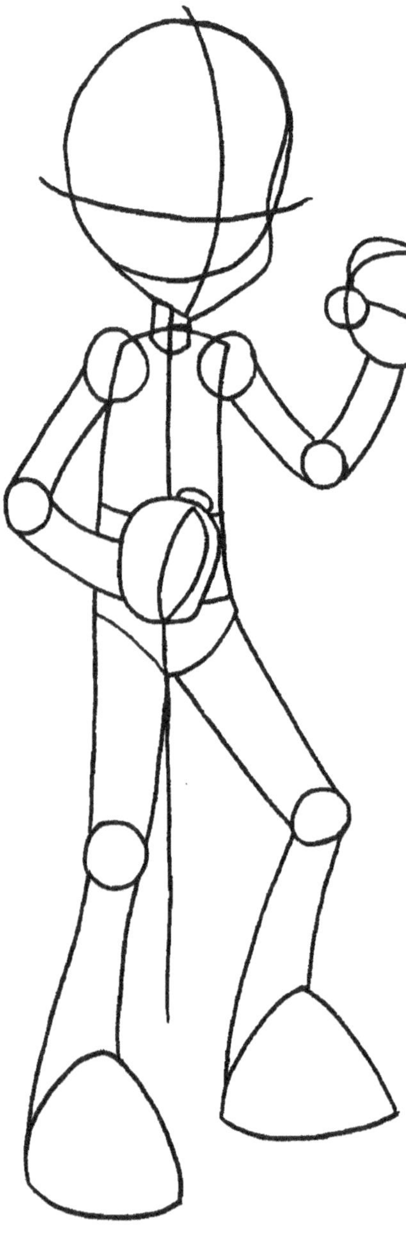

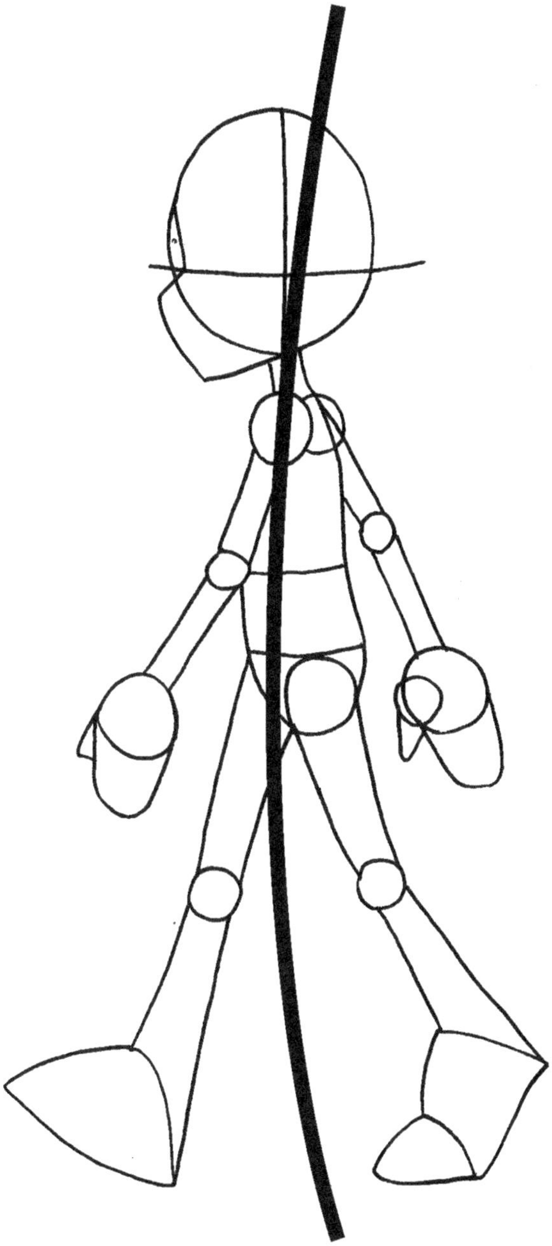

When a character is walking, the guideline is nearly straight.

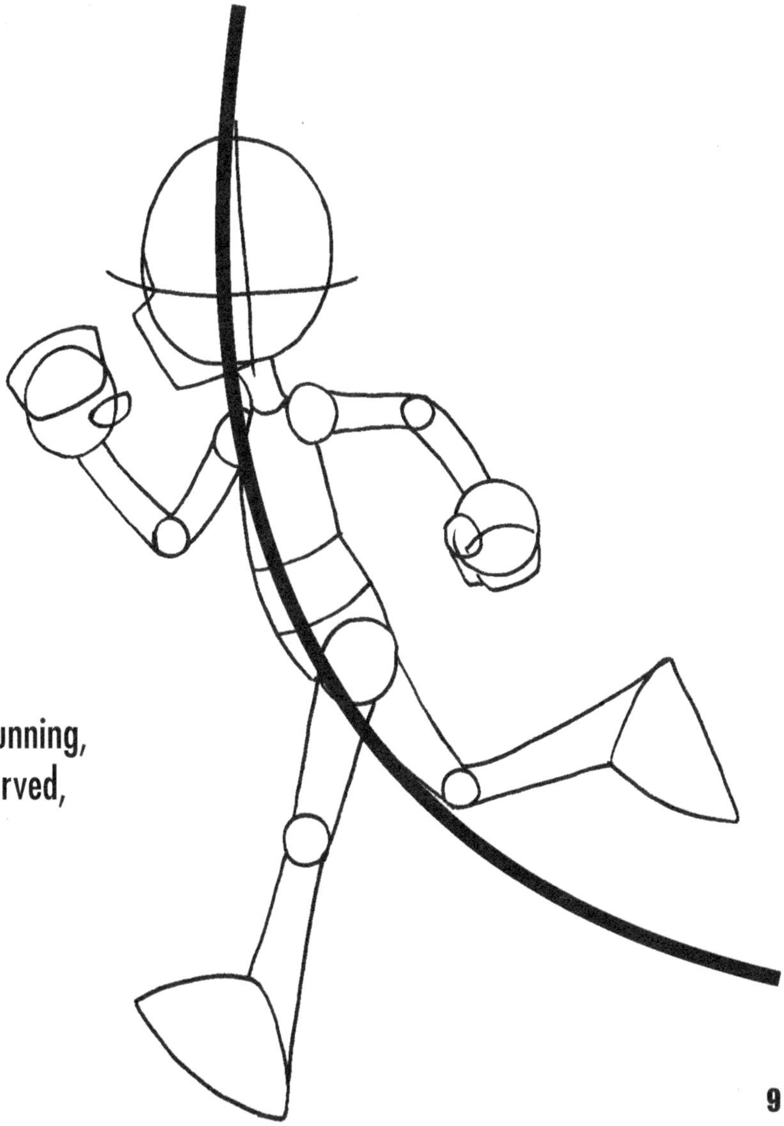

When the character is running, the guideline is more curved, to show movement.

HANDS

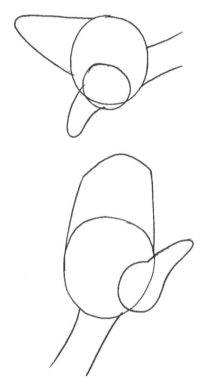

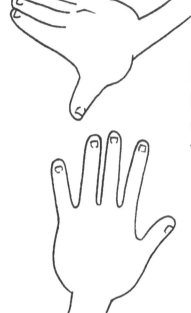

Draw a circle to indicate the palm of the hand. Sketch an outline of the area where you will draw the fingers.

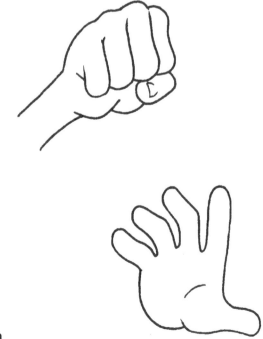

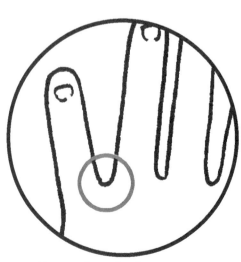

Notice that the fingers are joined by a small curved line.

FEET

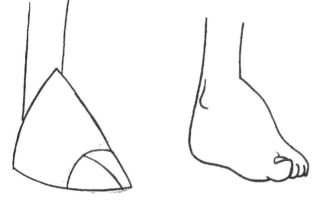

Sketch the feet using triangles as your reference.

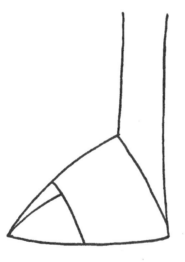

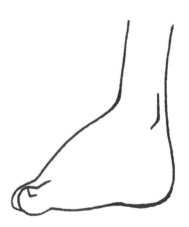

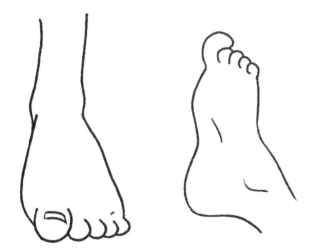

You can use your own feet as a reference when you practice drawing.

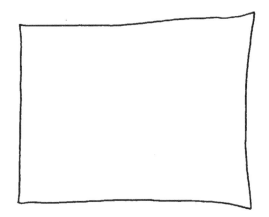

CLOTHES

To draw clothing, you must think about how fabric flows and adapts to different shapes.

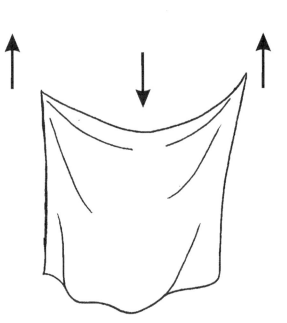

Use a towel to practice. Watch how it takes on different shapes, and try drawing them.

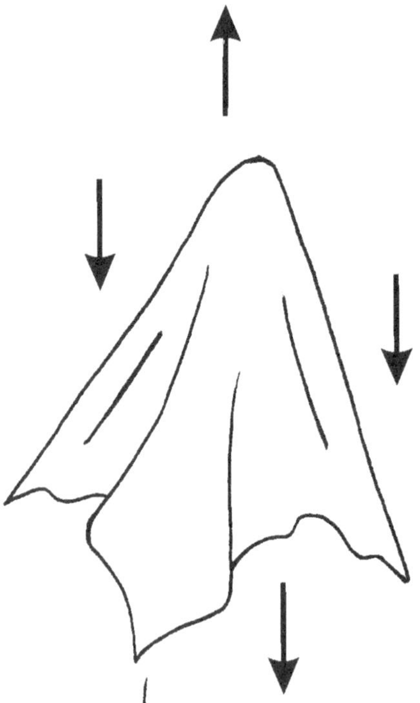

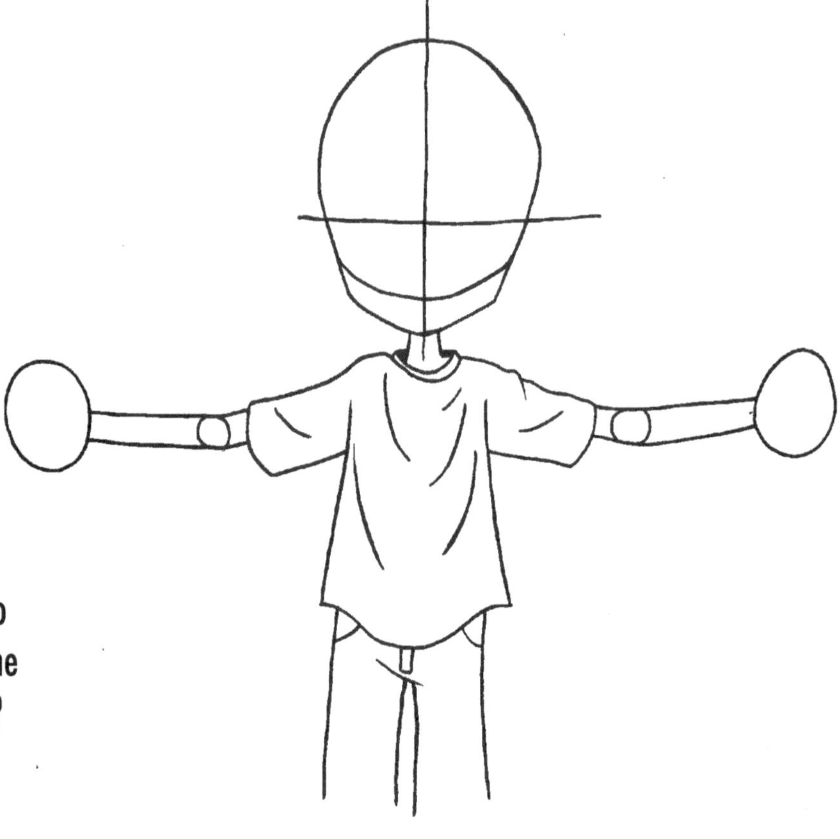

Consider how clothes adapt to your character's body. Does he wear baggy or tight clothing?

CHAPTER 2
The Heroes

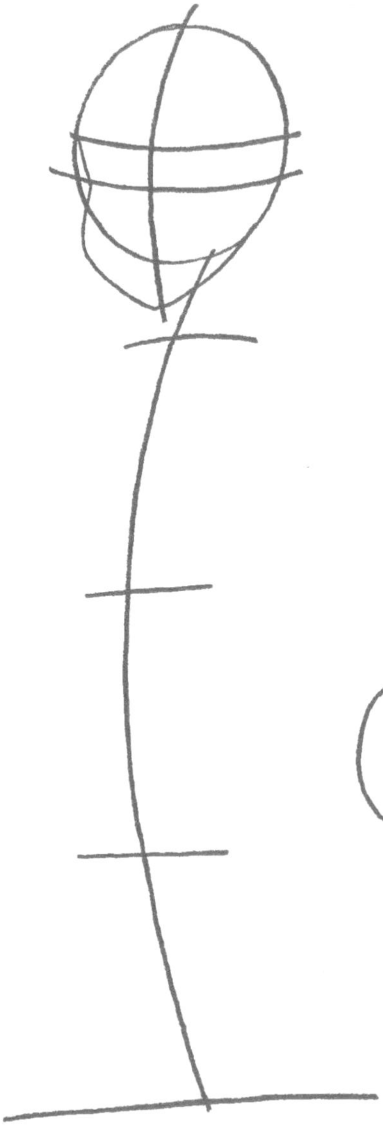

This character is four "heads" tall.

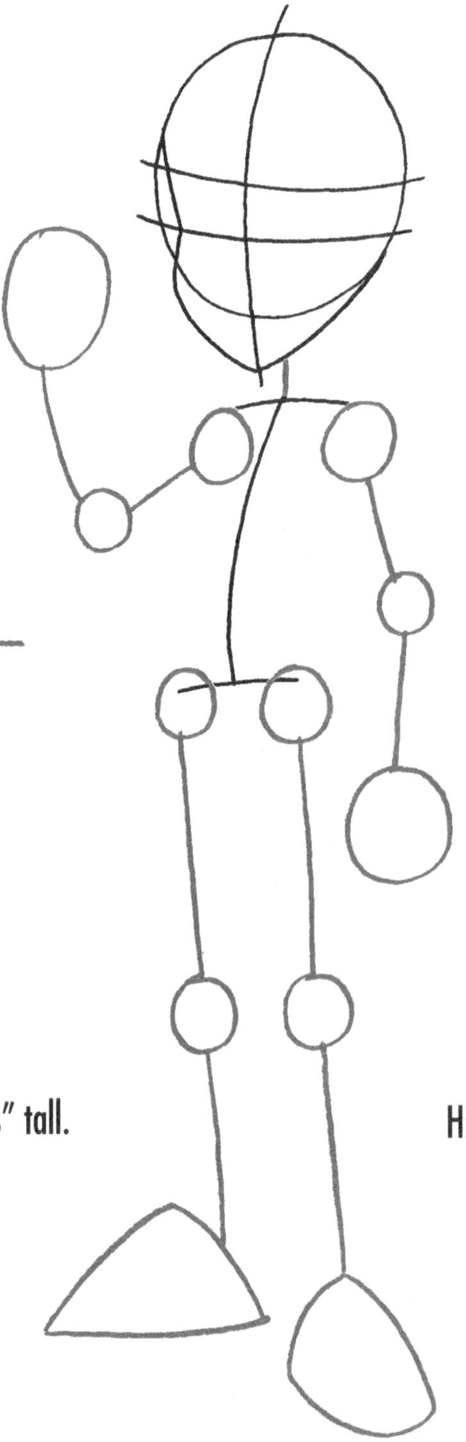

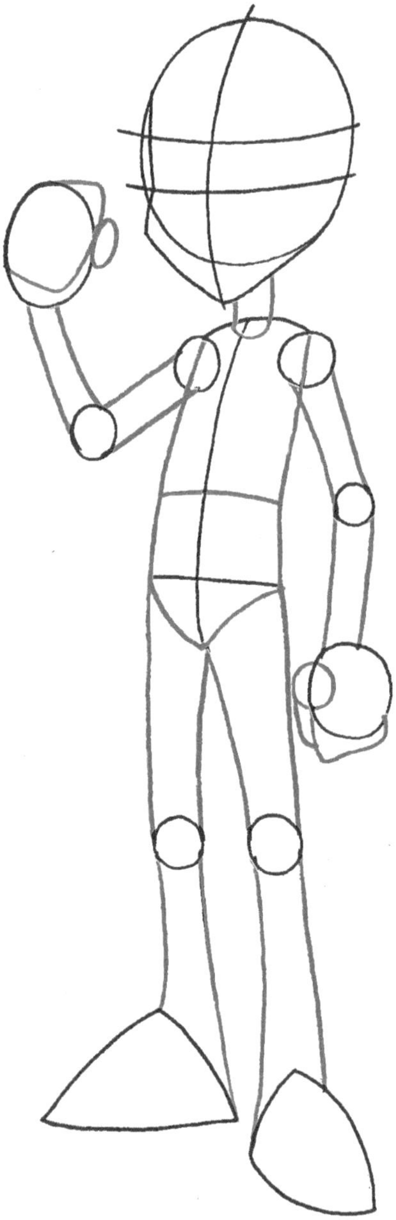

His body is strong and flexible.

HERO 1

His clothing indicates that he is a character who competes until the end.

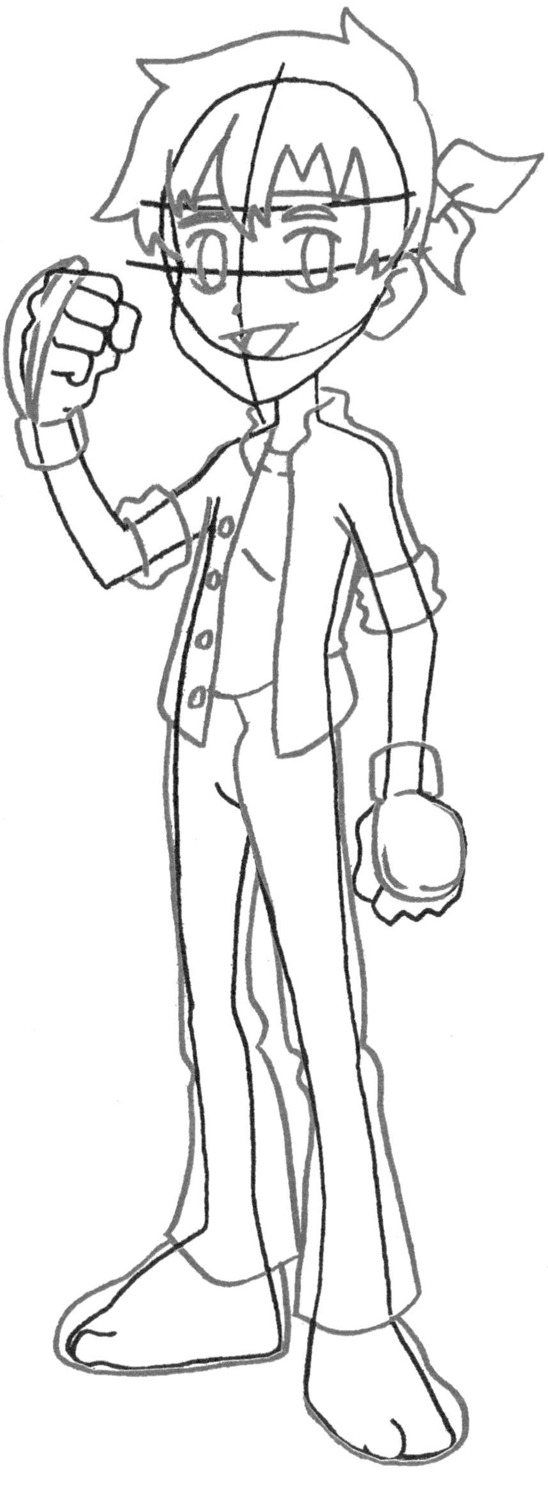

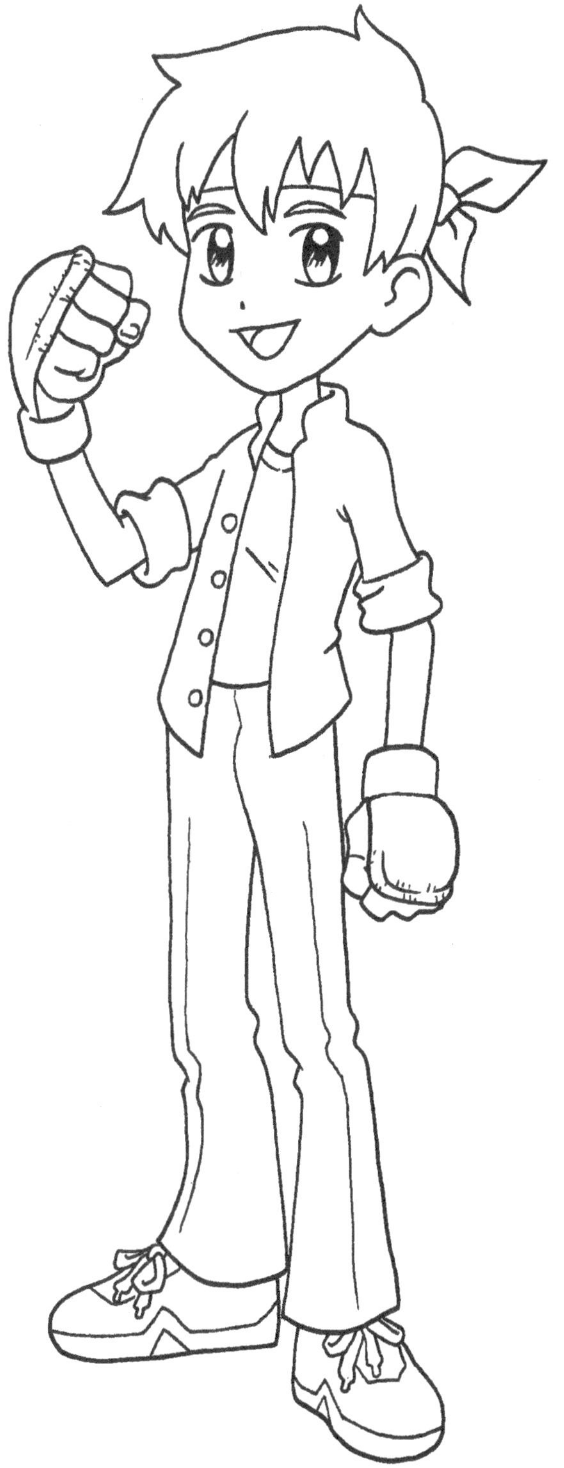

He wears the art-school uniform, but some details, such as his gloves and headband, give him a martial-arts look.

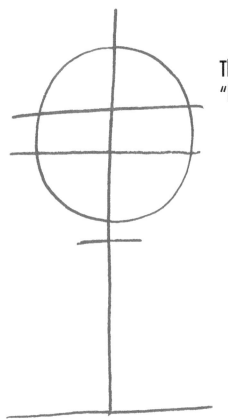

This character is two "heads" tall.

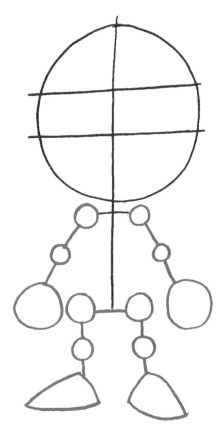

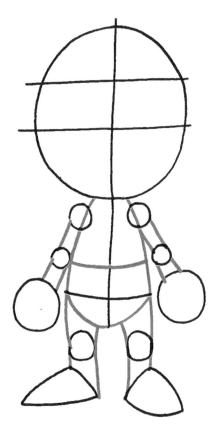

His body is small. He is elderly but hides his great power. His wisdom makes him strong.

HERO 2

His clothes indicate that he is a martial-arts master. Notice the shoes and jacket.

His eyebrows, mustache, and beard give him a wise look, and his long hair reflects his experience as a martial-arts master.

This character is four-and-a-half “heads” tall.

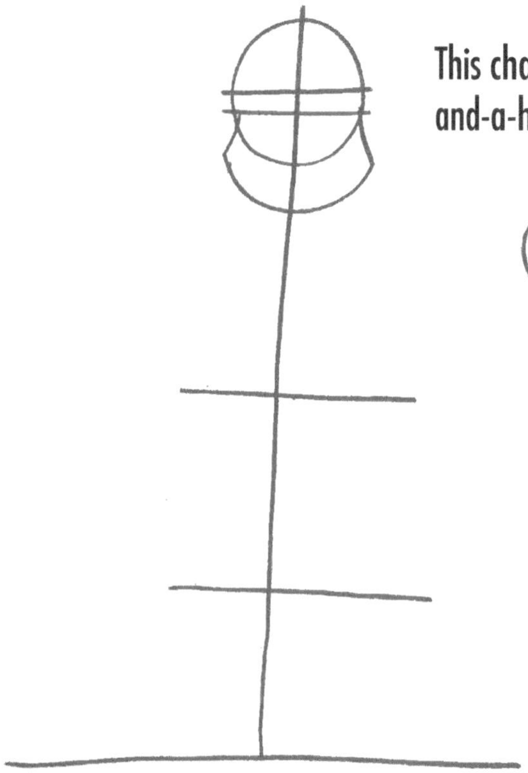

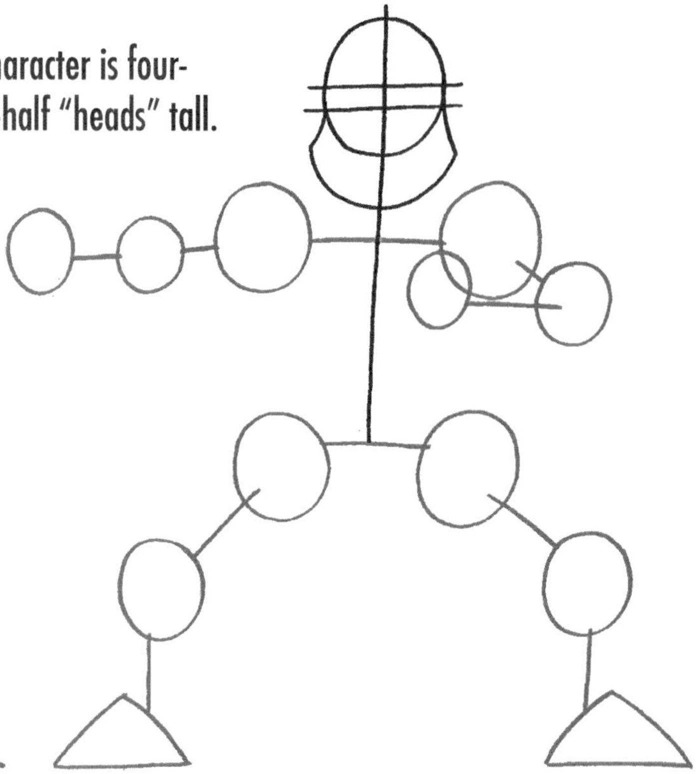

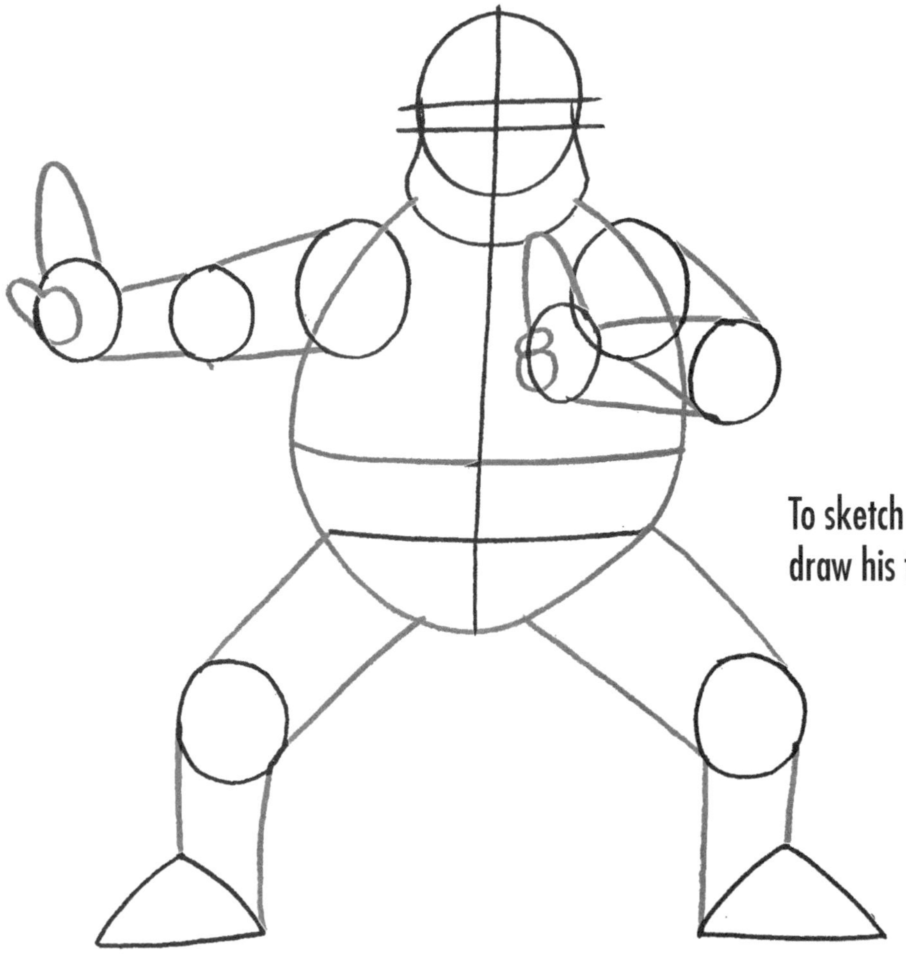

To sketch his body structure, draw his torso as an egg shape.

HERO 3

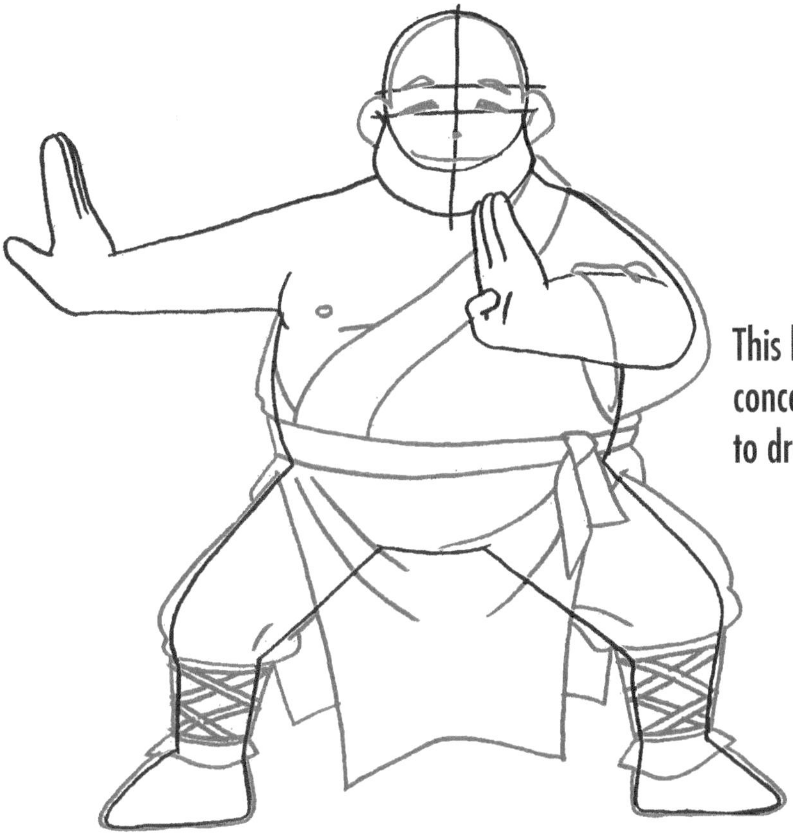

This big character is crouching—concentrating and getting ready to draw.

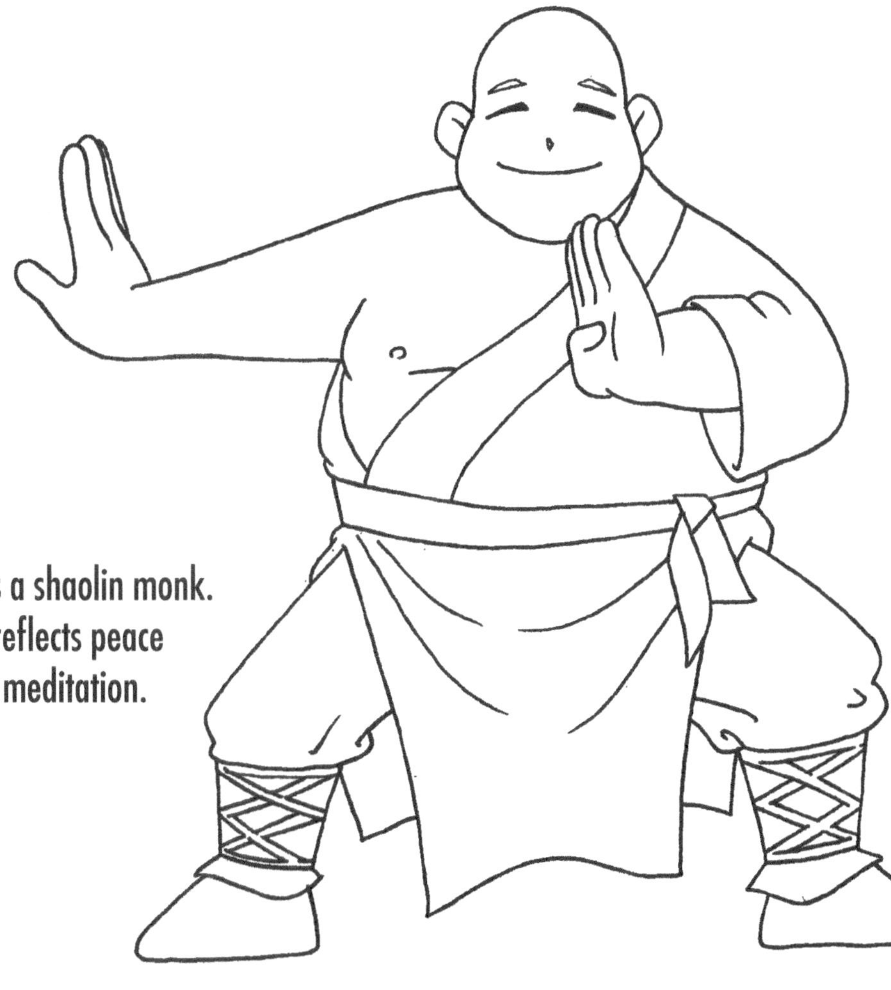

He is dressed as a shaolin monk. His expression reflects peace gained through meditation.

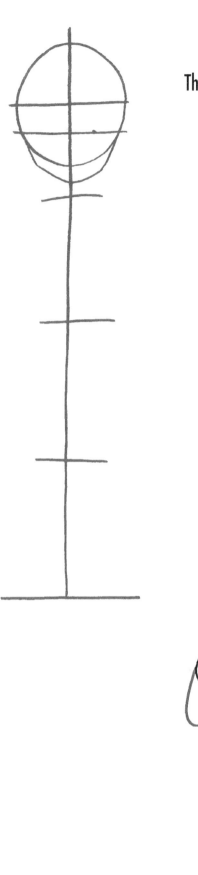

This character is four "heads" tall.

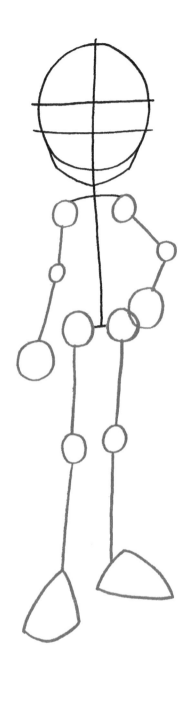

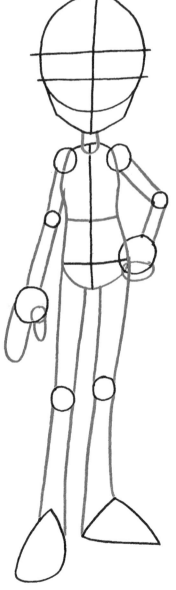

Her body is agile and flexible.

HERO 4

Her clothing combines a dress and sportswear.
This allows her to be both stylish and comfortable.

This charming girl is always willing
to help those in need.

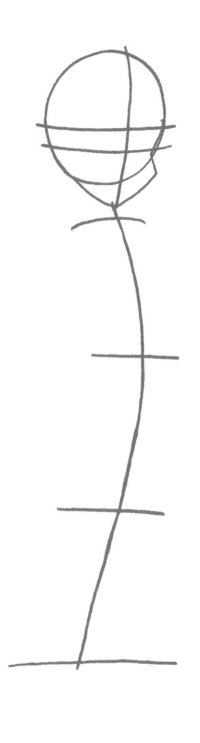

This character is four "heads" tall.

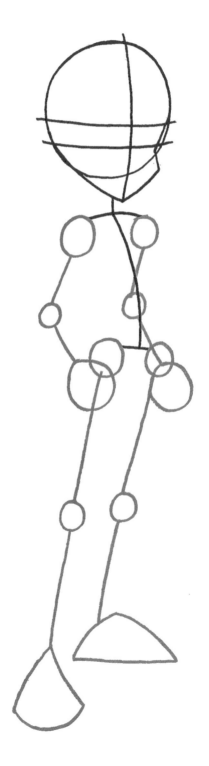

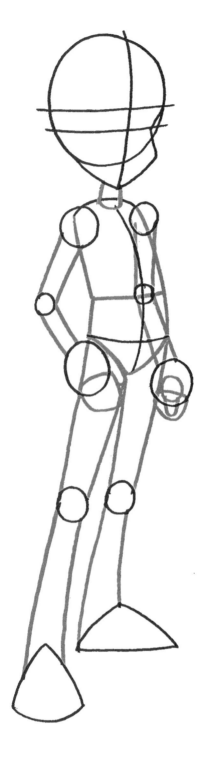

His pose suggests that
he is confident and
feels like a winner.

HERO 5

He is concerned about fashion and always tries to look his best. He picks elegant clothing and enjoys wearing glasses.

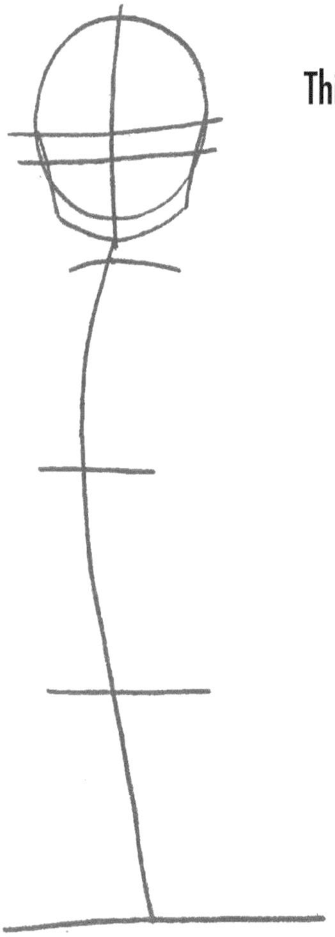

This character is four "heads" tall.

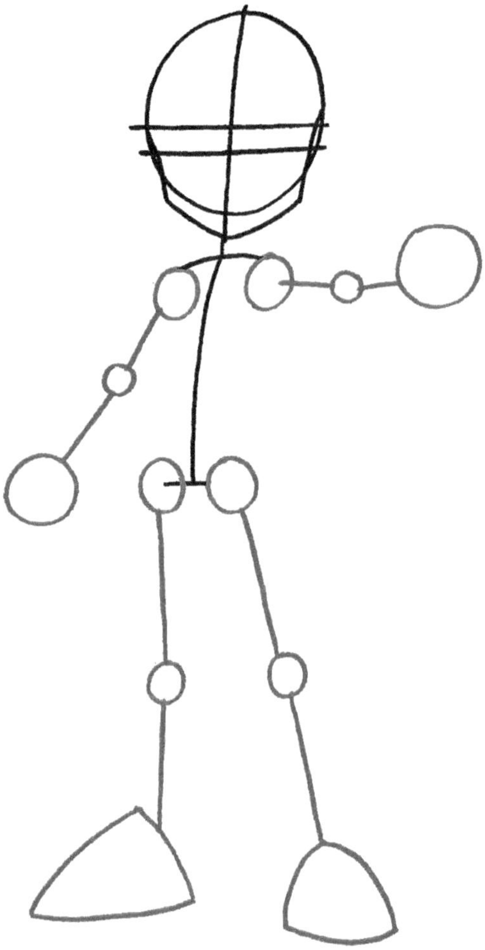

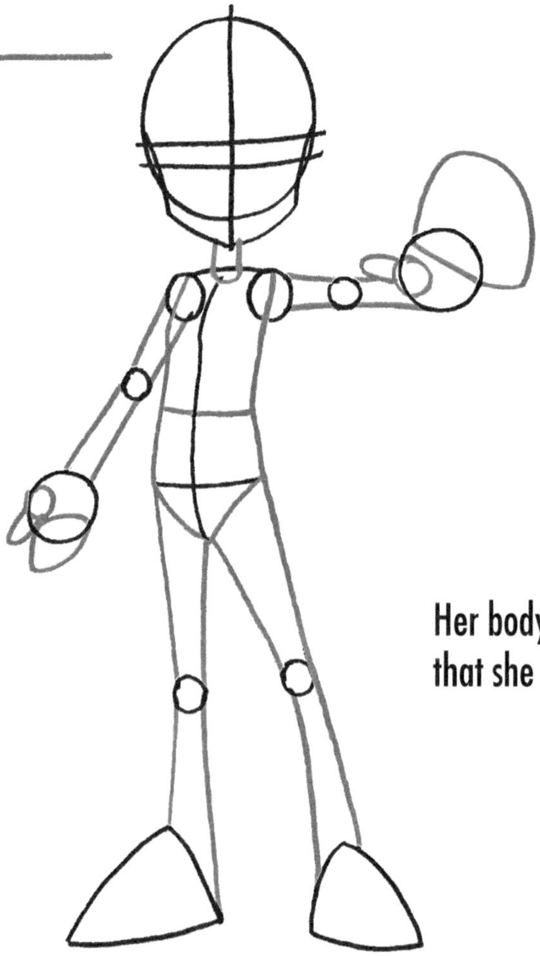

Her body conveys a powerful flow of energy that she uses to create masterpieces.

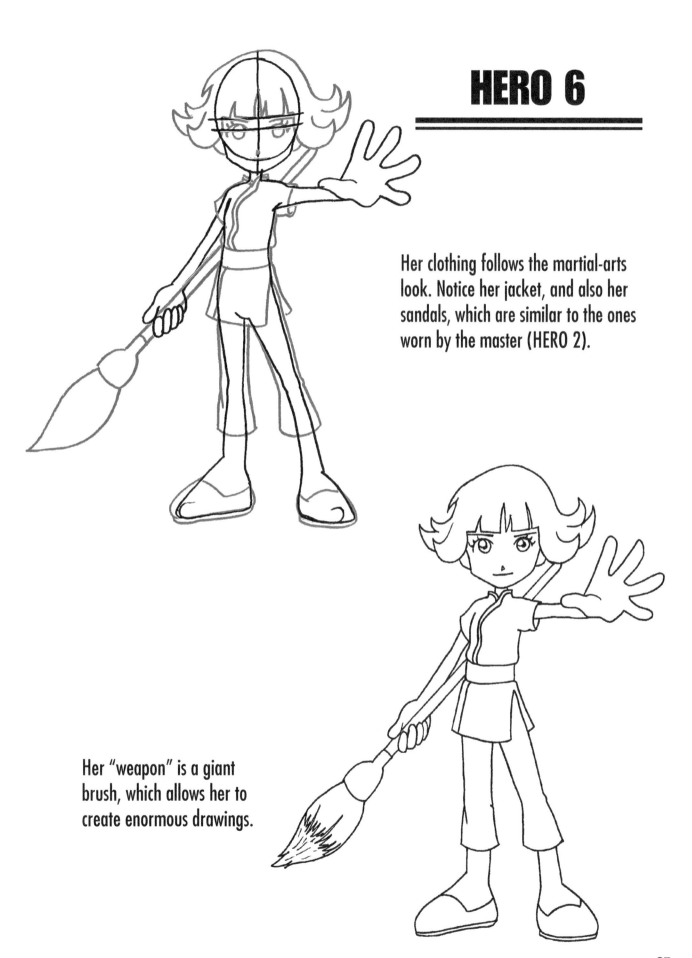

HERO 6

Her clothing follows the martial-arts look. Notice her jacket, and also her sandals, which are similar to the ones worn by the master (HERO 2).

Her "weapon" is a giant brush, which allows her to create enormous drawings.

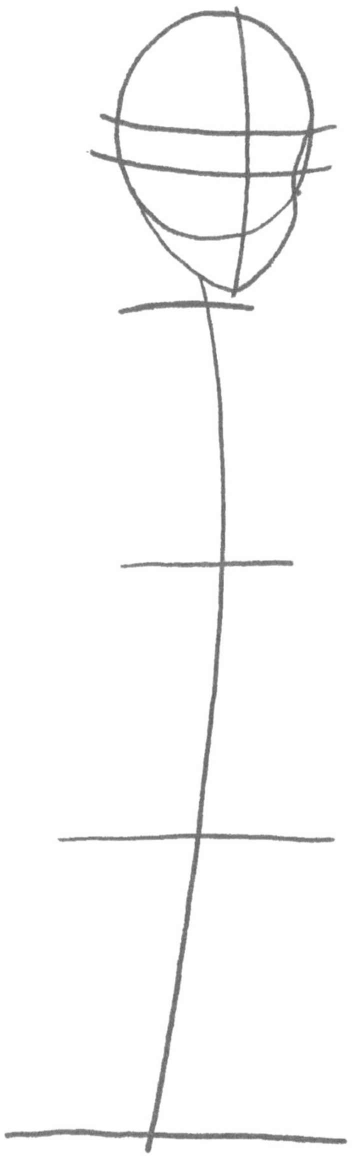

This character is four "heads" tall.

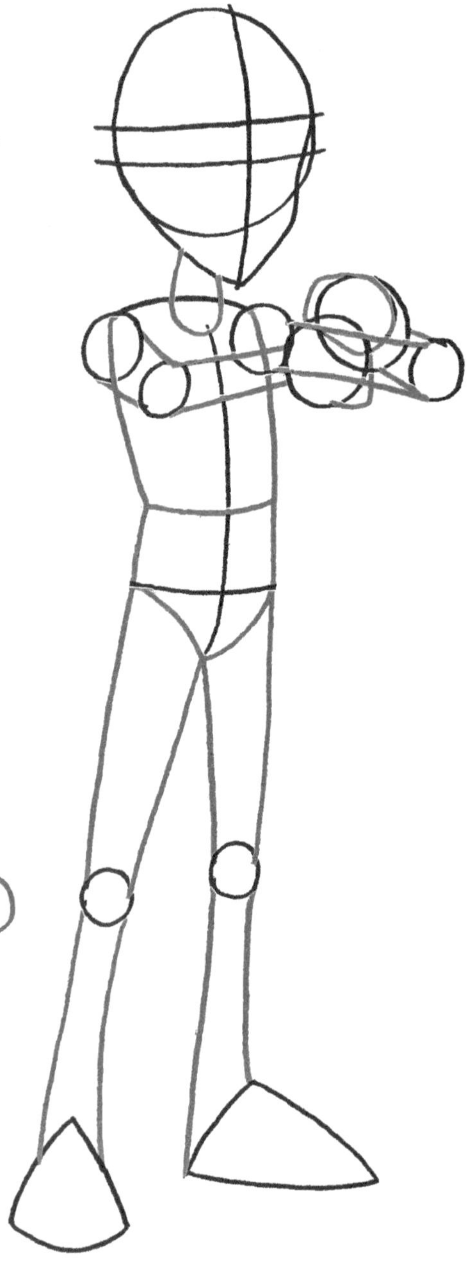

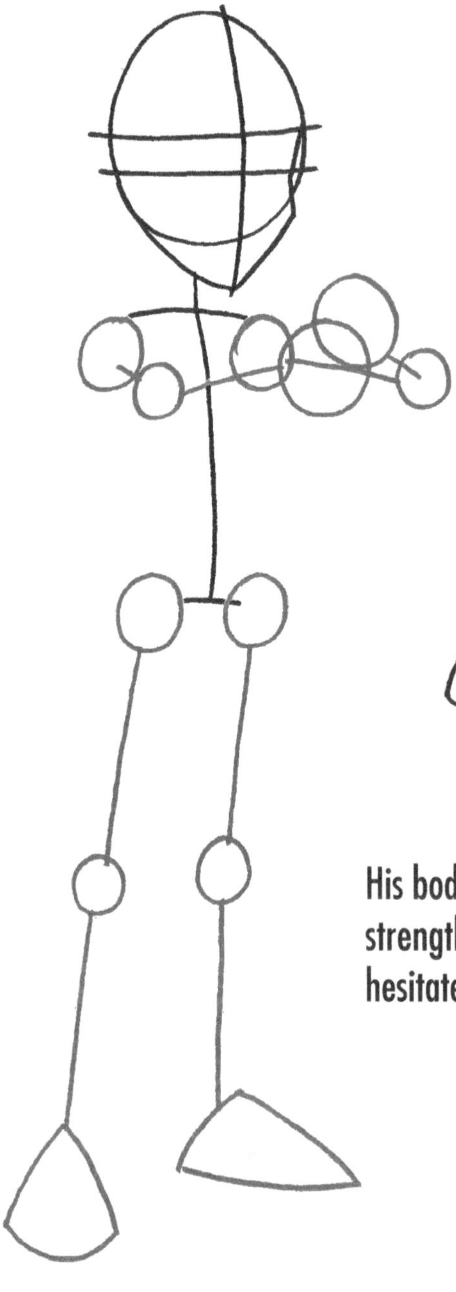

His body gives the impression of strength and power. He doesn't hesitate in the face of danger.

HERO 7

He wears a ponytail and has an eye patch covering a battle scar.

Although he only has the use of one eye, he is a great artist.

He wears an outfit that shows he is a tough fighter. His shirt and pants are torn, and his hands and feet are covered with bandages for protection.

HERO 8

Here is the art-school mascot — always willing to get into trouble while the students are learning new drawing techniques!

This character is three "heads" tall.

Art School
Backgrounds

Backgrounds: Indoors

By combining simple geometric figures and adding details, we can create interesting objects.

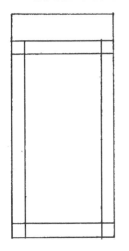 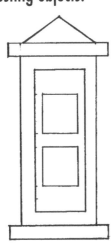 

1. Sketch an outline using squares and rectangles.

2. Draw the final shape.

3. Add details.

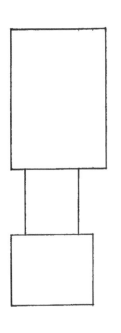 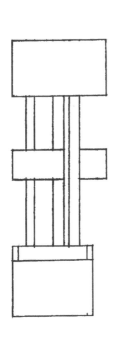 

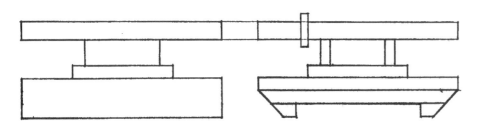 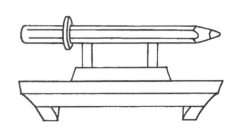

Step 1: Draw the floor and walls of this room, where we will place our characters and objects.

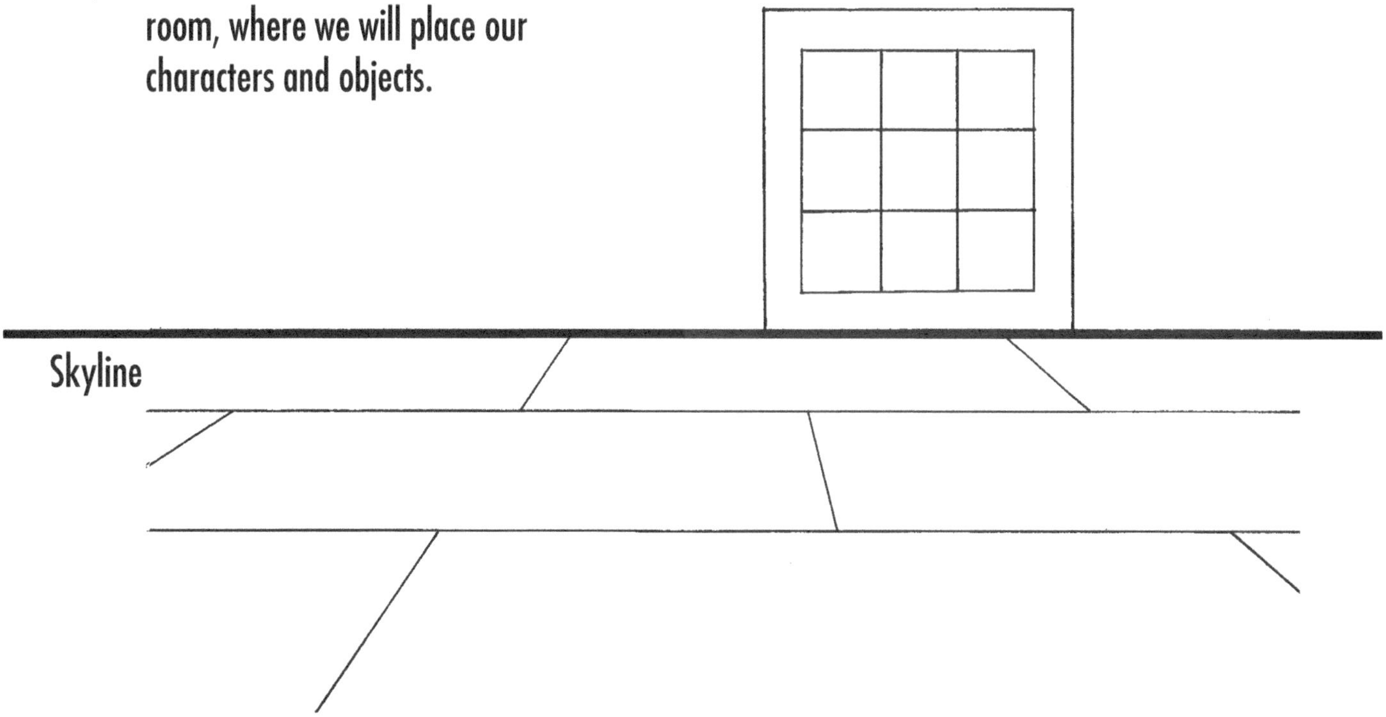

Skyline

Tip

The skyline marks where the ground ends and the sky begins. It also draws the eye into the picture.

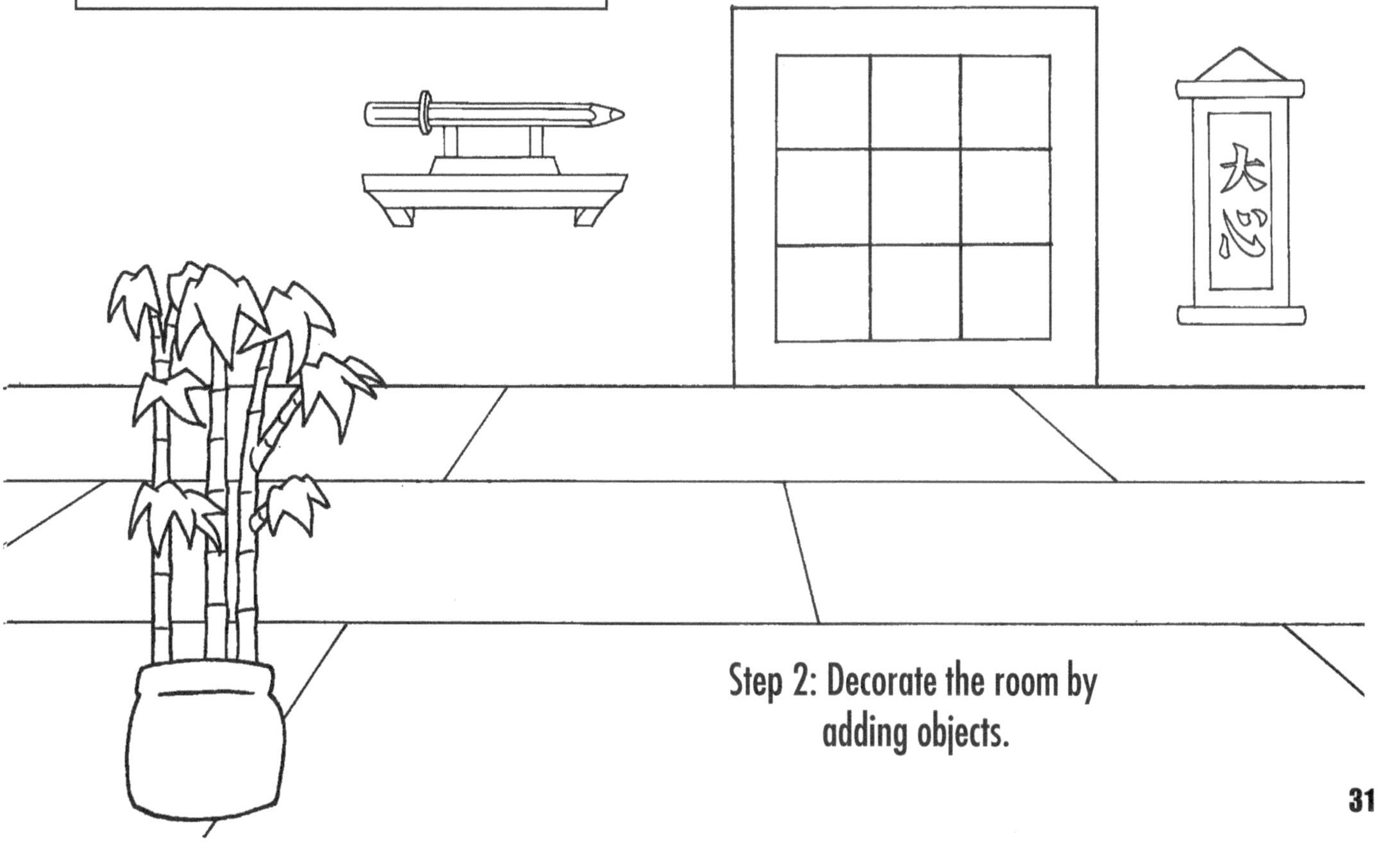

Step 2: Decorate the room by adding objects.

Backgrounds: Outdoors

Tree

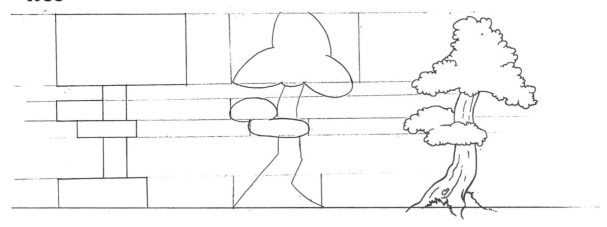

School

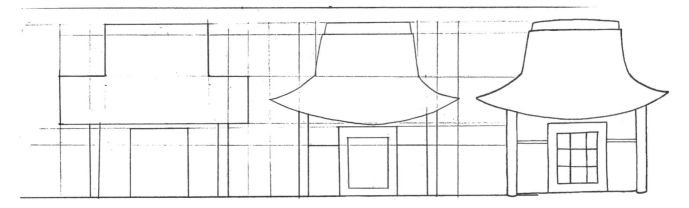

Rock

It is important that our characters have a place to live out their adventures.

Background objects in the outdoors are drawn with less detail when they are far away.

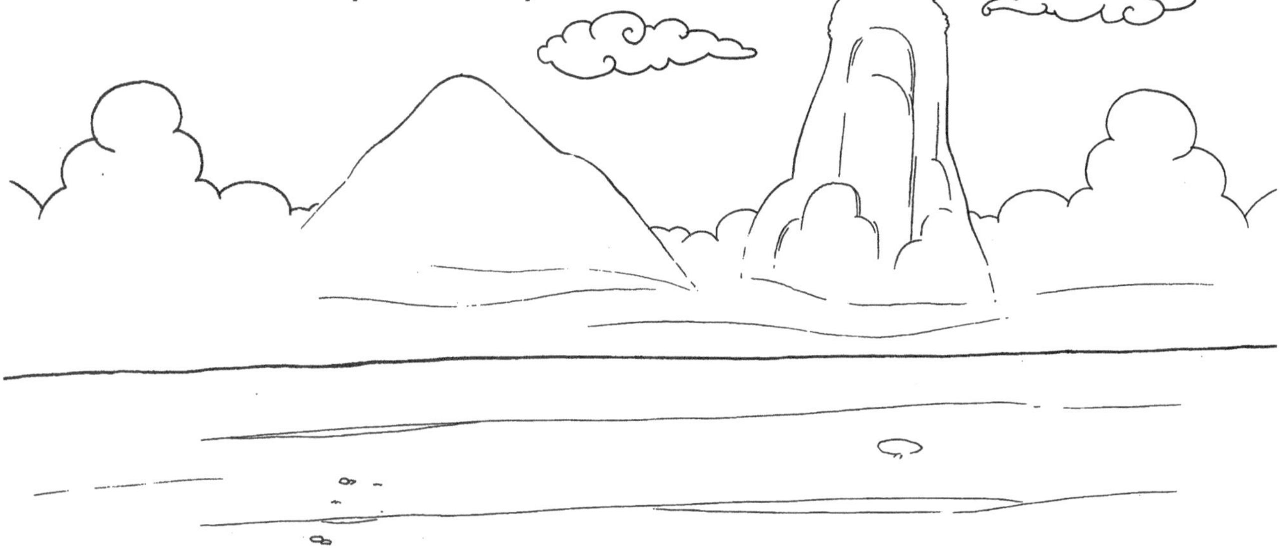

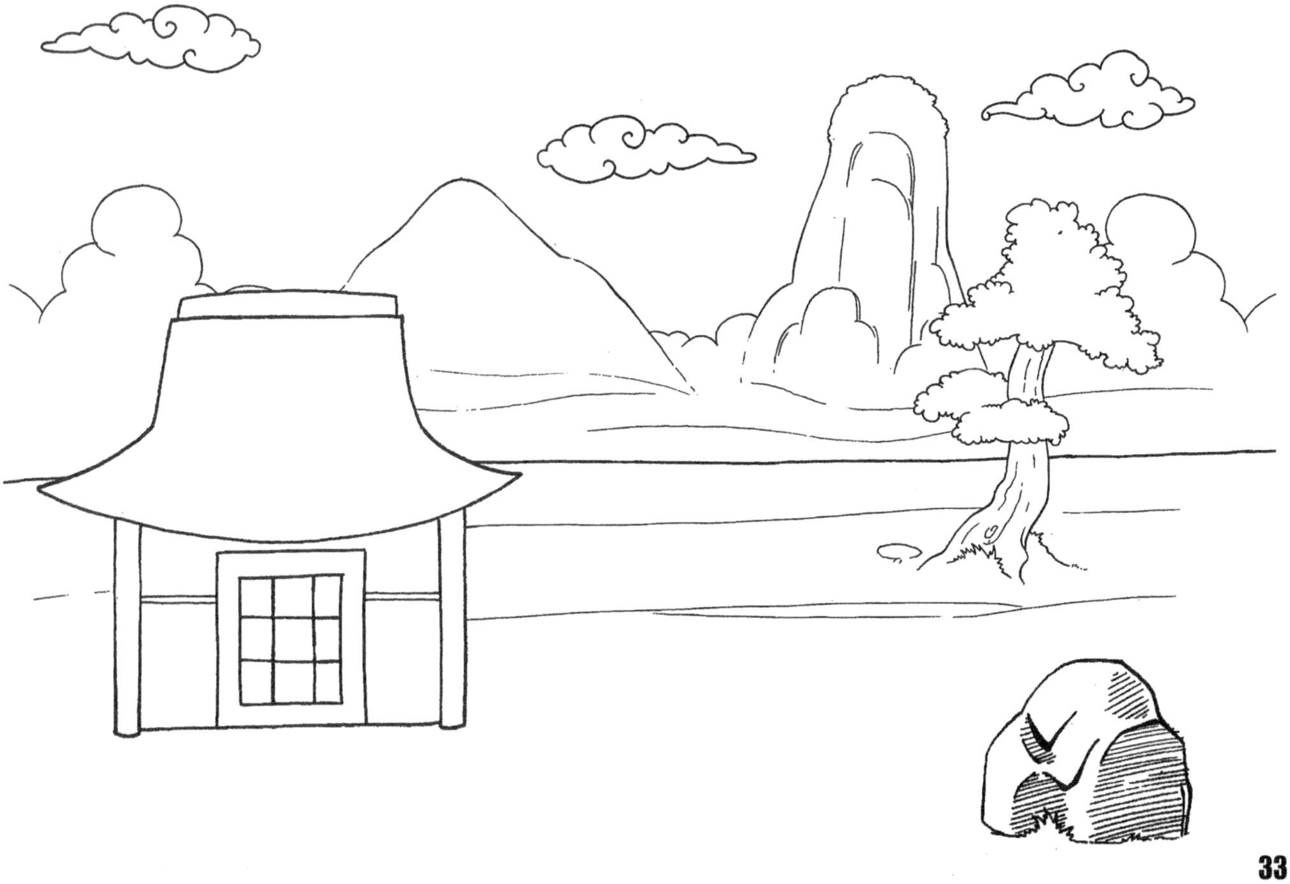

Perspective

Perspective is a visual effect used in drawing to represent a three-dimensional (3-D) image in two dimensions (2-D). It allows us to generate the illusion of depth.

Characters or objects of the same height, standing in line, are drawn with the same level of detail.

Depth affects size and detail. Characters who are standing in front are larger and more detailed than characters standing towards the back.

Let's see the second image above from the side. Notice how the characters are positioned. Creating a composition is, in some ways, like taking a photograph.

CHAPTER 3
The Villains

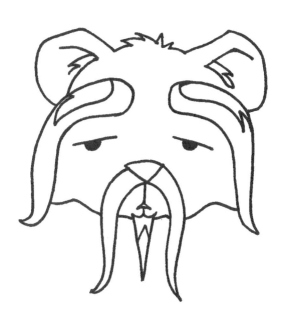

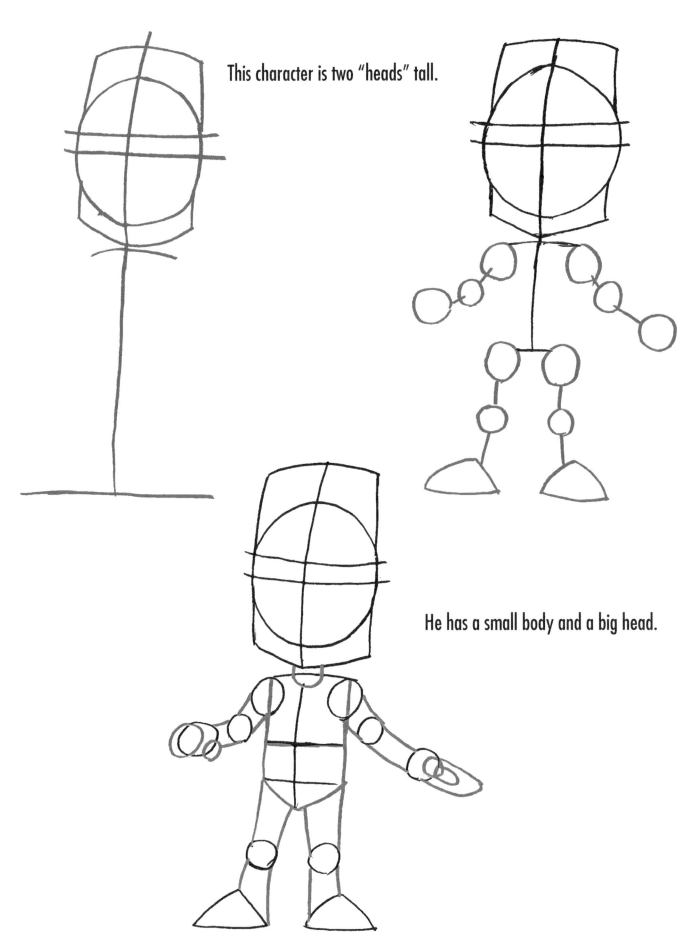

This character is two "heads" tall.

He has a small body and a big head.

VILLAIN 1

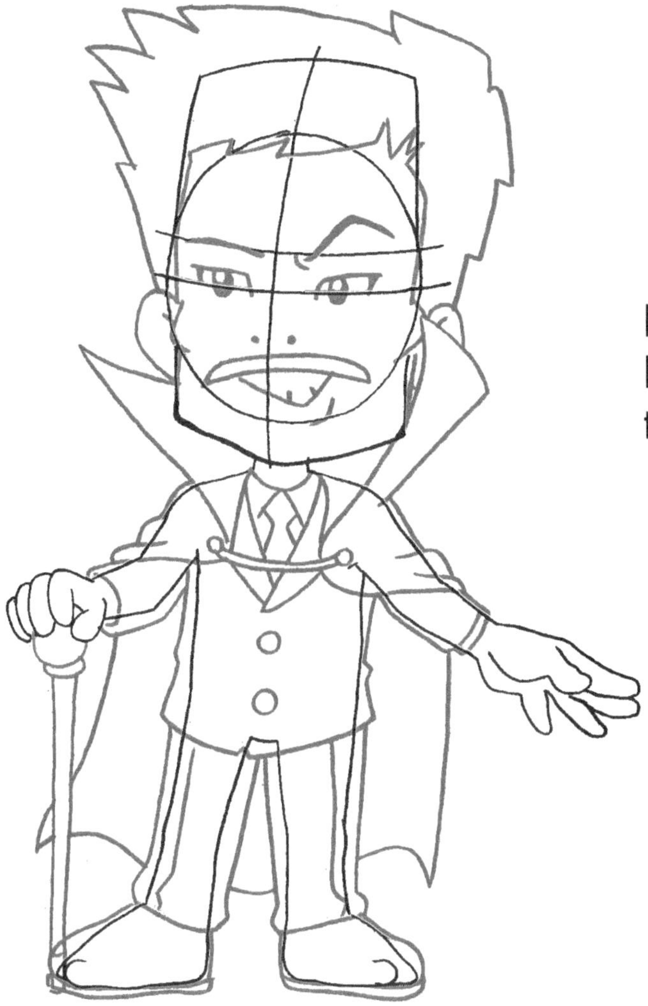

His high forehead suggests a vast intelligence. His left eyebrow is arched to show that he is thinking of something evil!

He is the villainous schoolmaster. He wears a cape and uses a cane. This villain thirsts for power.

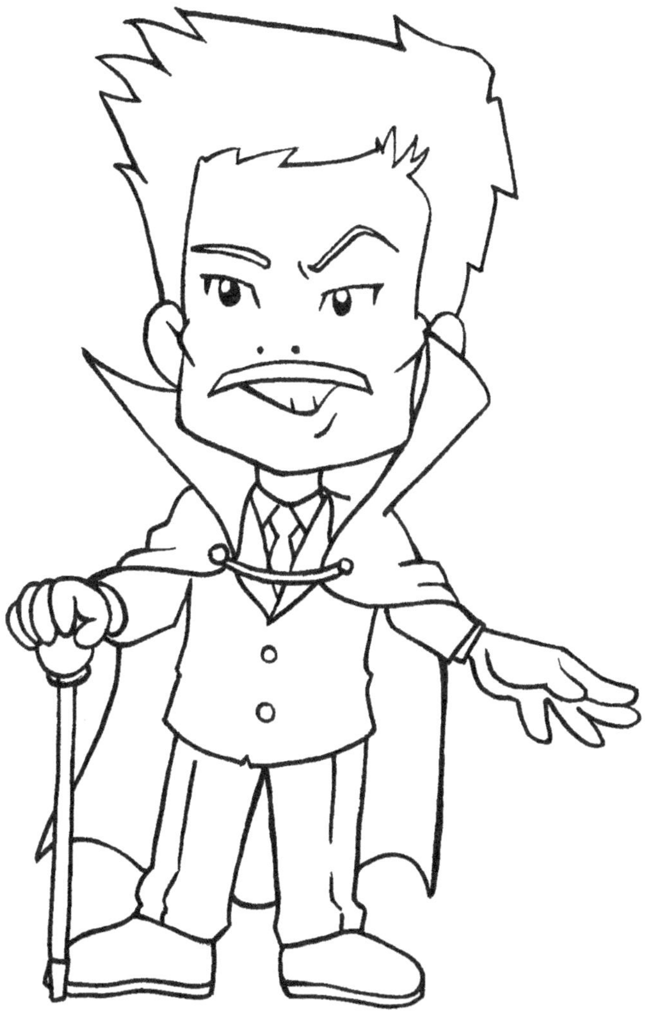

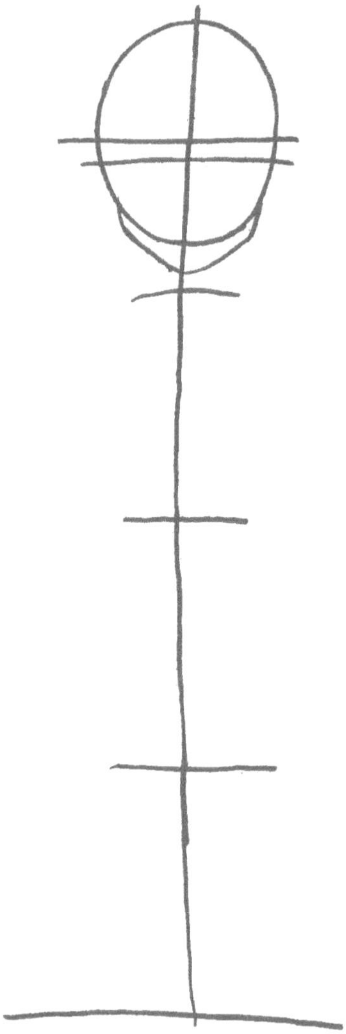

This character is four "heads" tall.

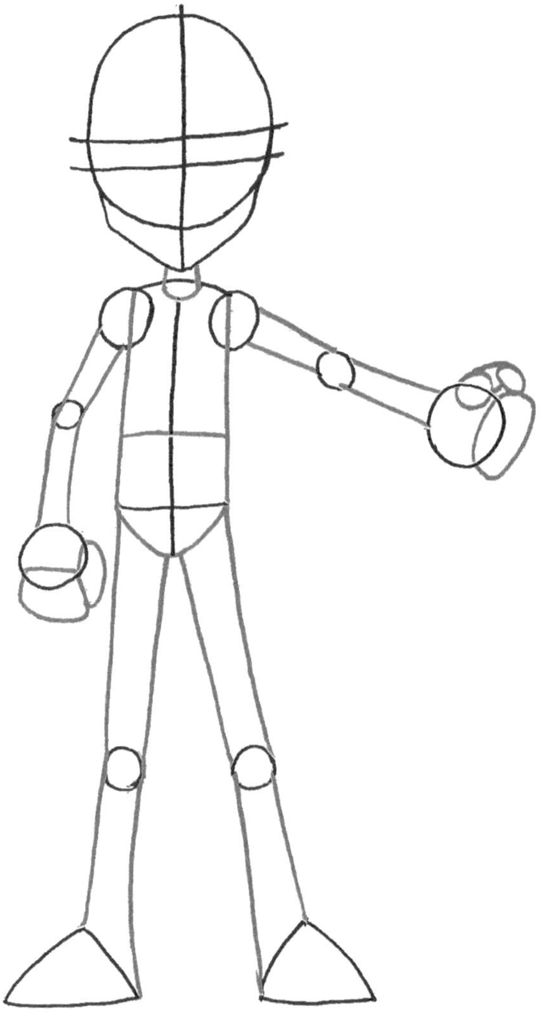

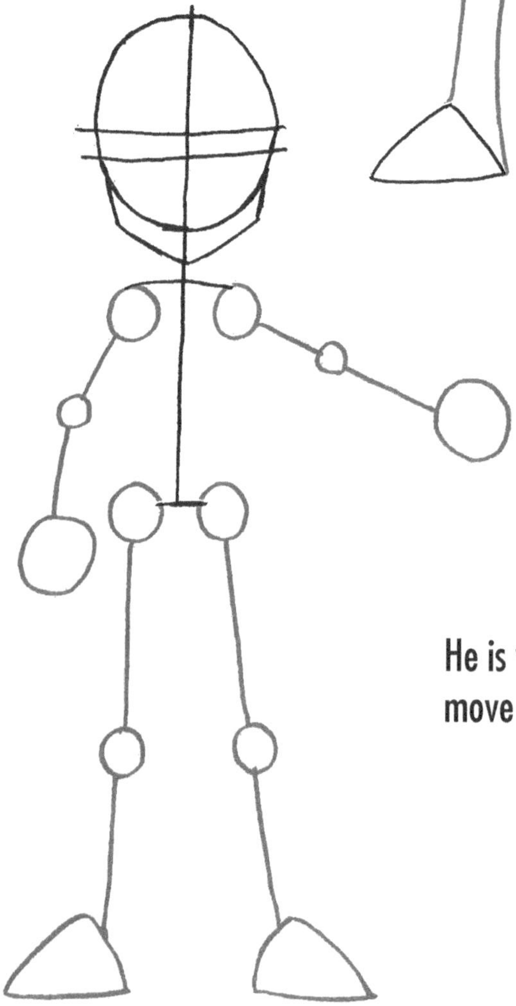

He is very thin—this allows him to move quickly when competing.

VILLAIN 2

His clothes are based on a ninja uniform. He conceals his identity with a mask.

His art-school weapon is a set square [t-square], which allows him to create perfect lines.

This character is two "heads" tall.

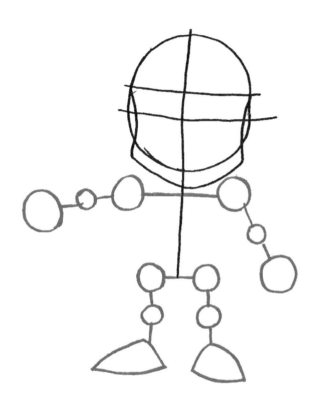

Her body is small and appears weak, but she knows how to do powerful magic.

VILLAIN 3

Her rubber cane can be used to erase our heroes' drawings.

She wears her white hair tied up.

This woman is an evil witch. She will use her powers to destroy the art-school students' drawings.

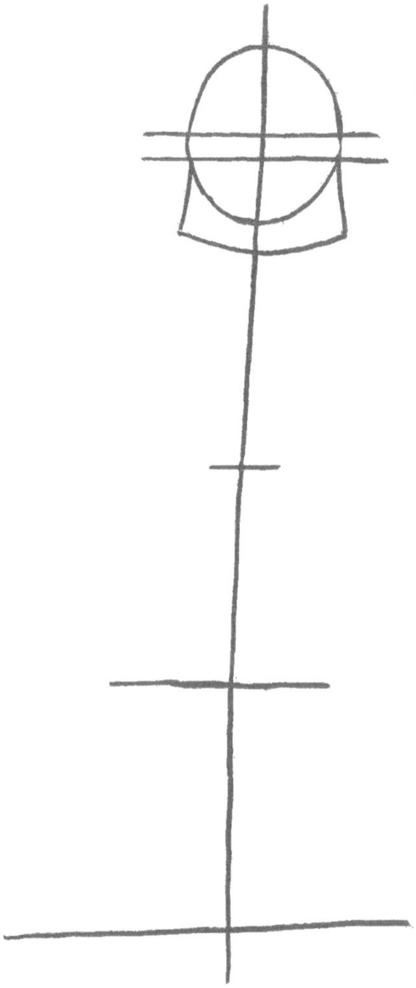

This character is four "heads" tall.

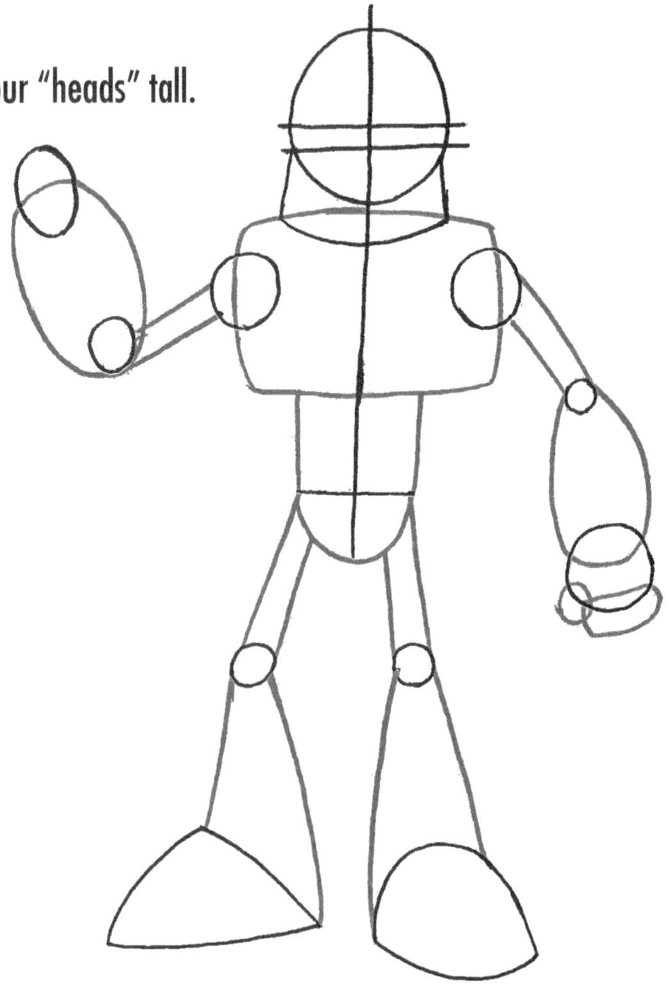

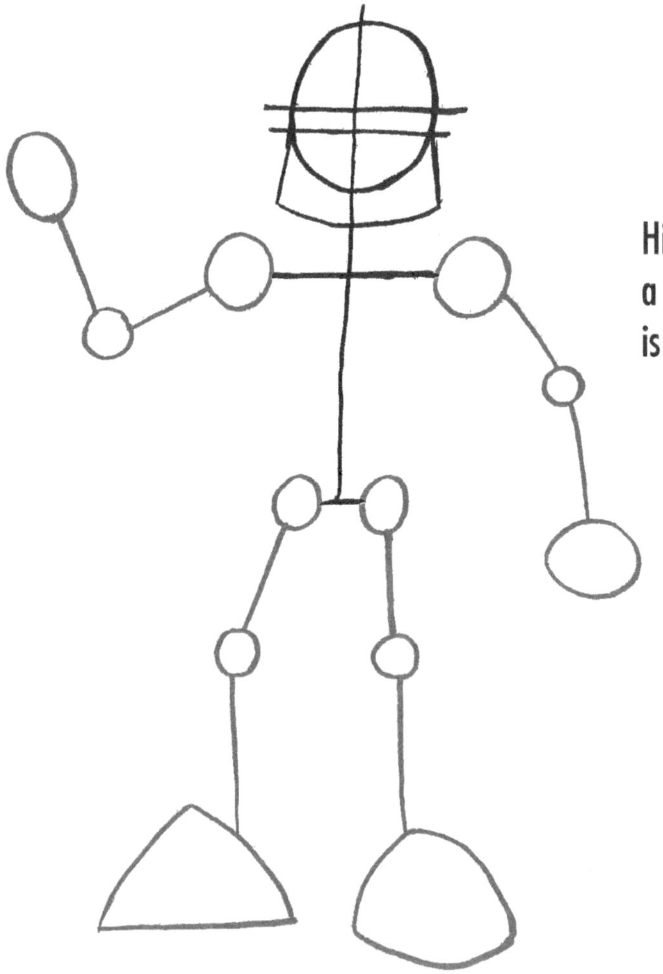

His metal torso is shaped like a big rectangle, and his waist is a thin column.

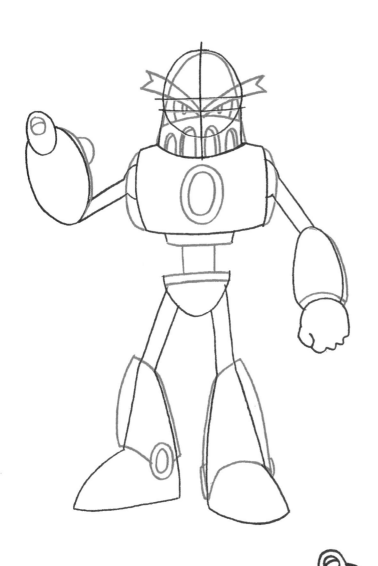

VILLAIN 4

All of this villain's details are made of metal. His energy source is located in his chest.

His right hand is a powerful electric pencil sharpener. He uses it to destroy the heroes' pencils.

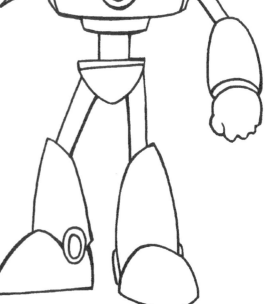

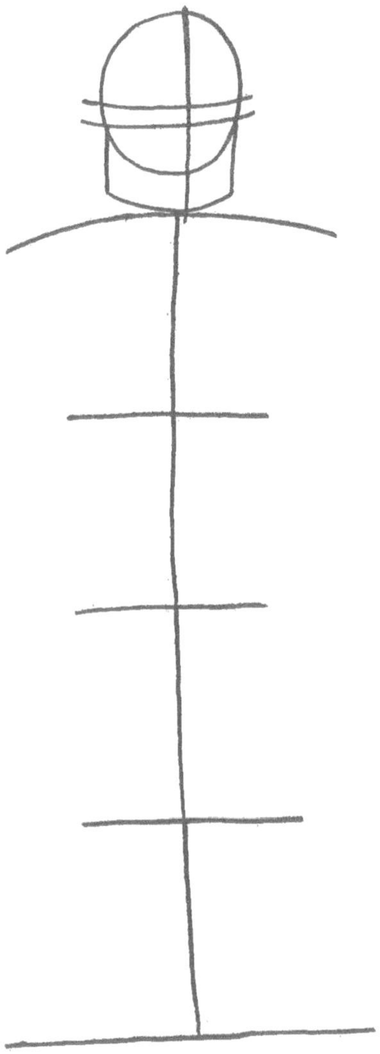

This character is five-and-a-half "heads" tall.

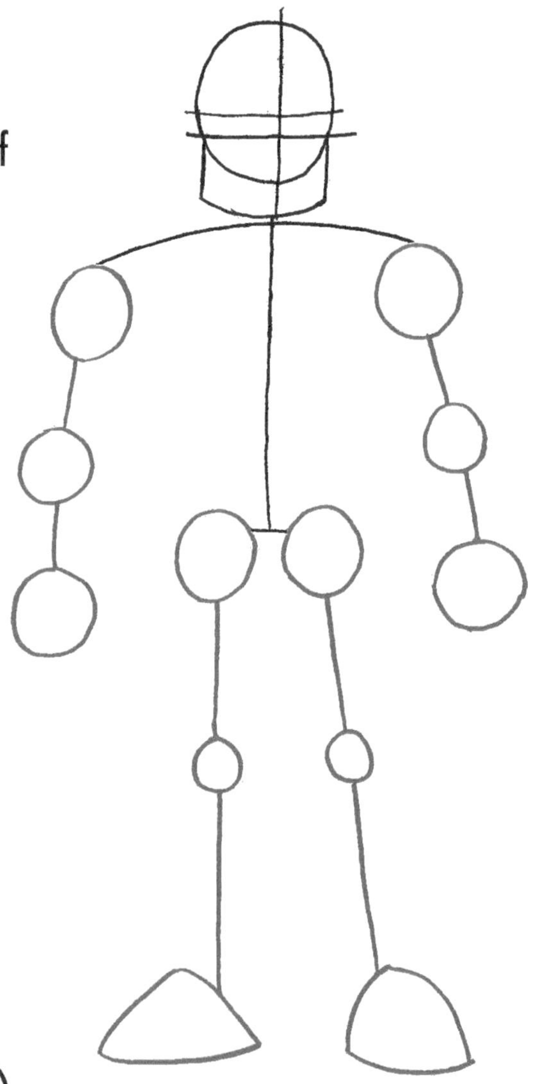

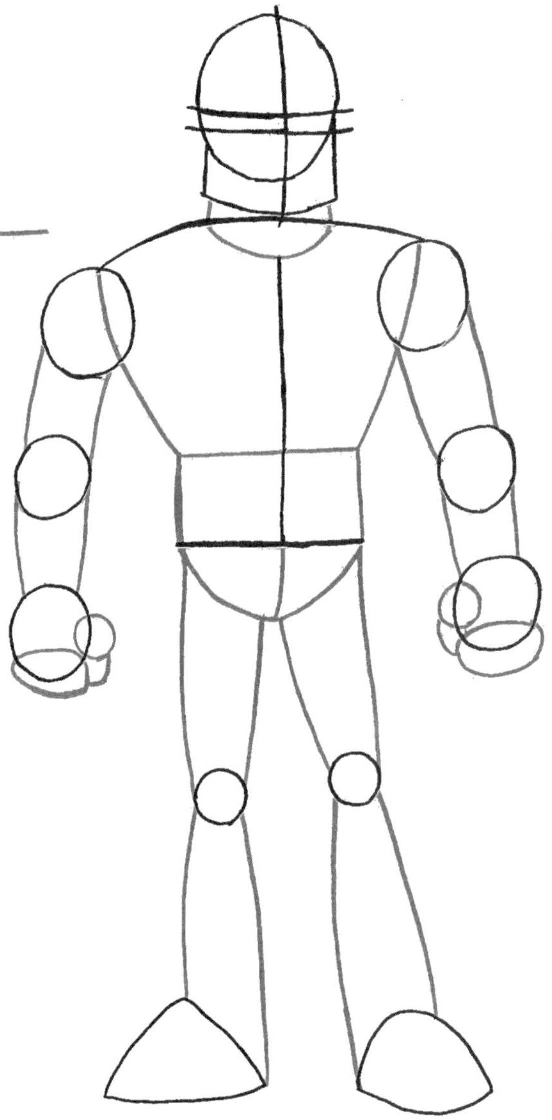

This character is pure muscle! His back is shaped like an upside-down triangle.

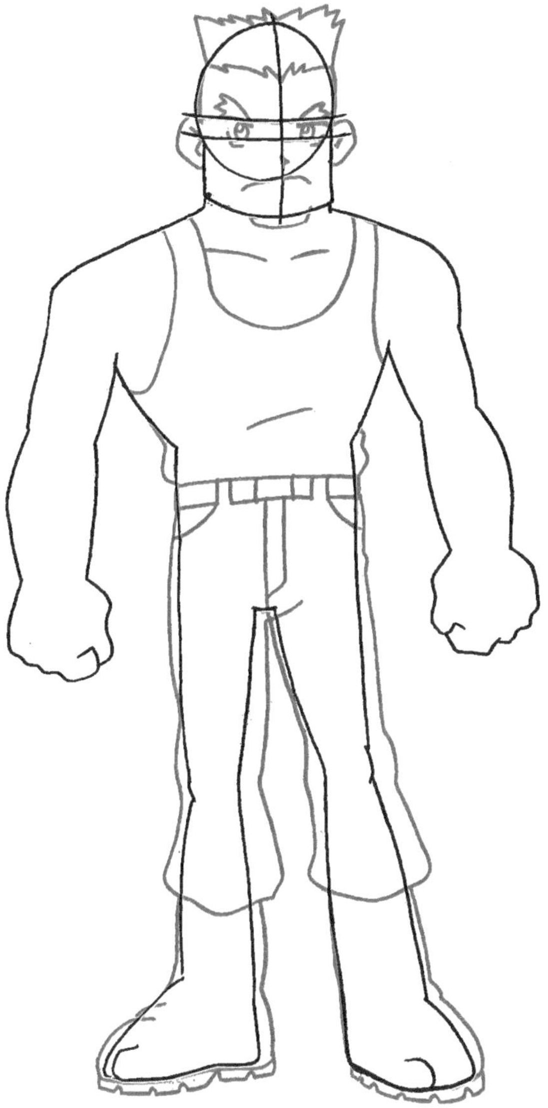

VILLAIN 5

He wears a tank top and military-style pants and boots. He wears his hair in a spiky cut.

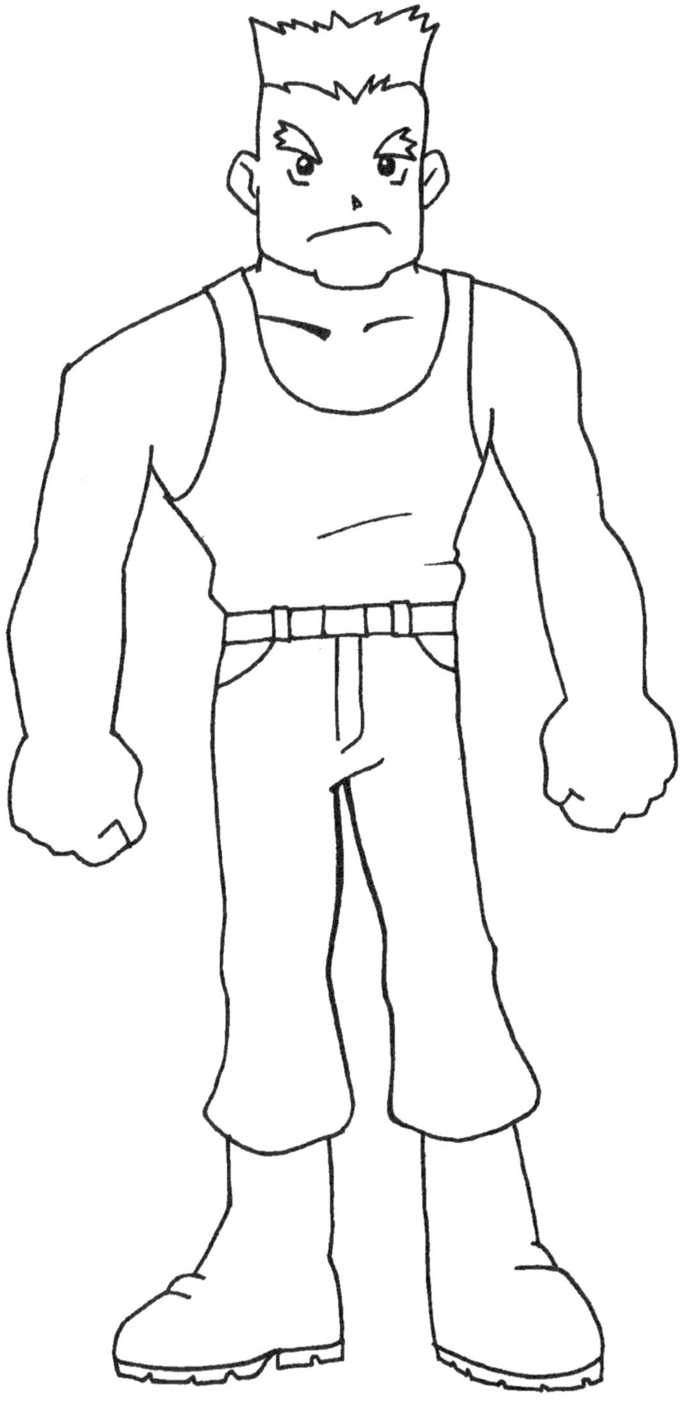

The evil master, who has developed this villain more for his muscles than his intelligence, controls his every move.

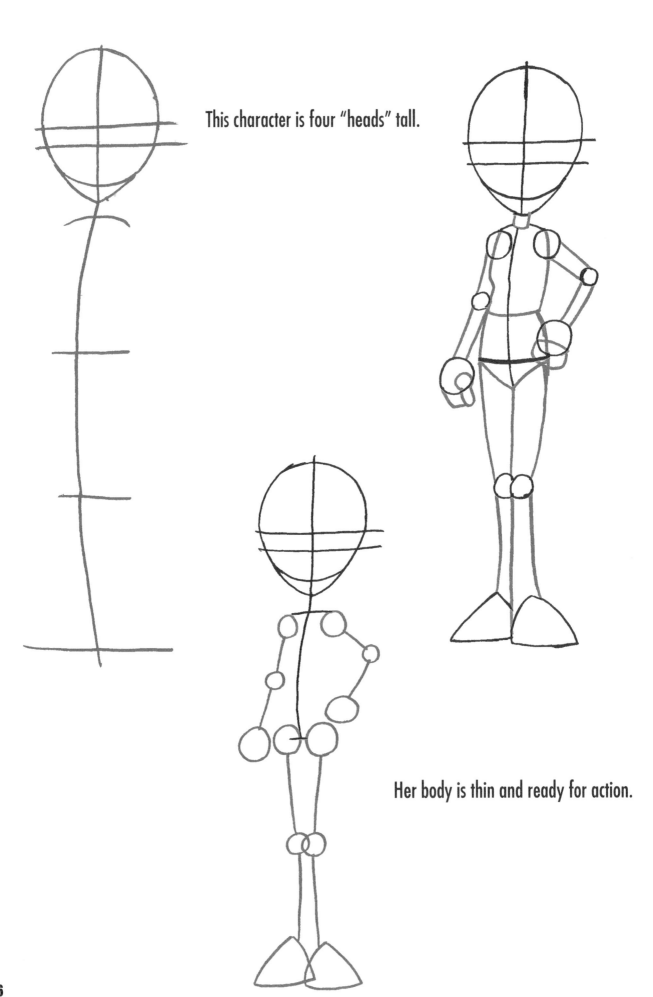

This character is four "heads" tall.

Her body is thin and ready for action.

VILLAIN 6

Her hair, clothing, and shoes reflect her dark, mysterious personality.

Beautiful on the outside, but evil on the inside, this villain has a secret technique: She spills ink on her opponents' drawings!

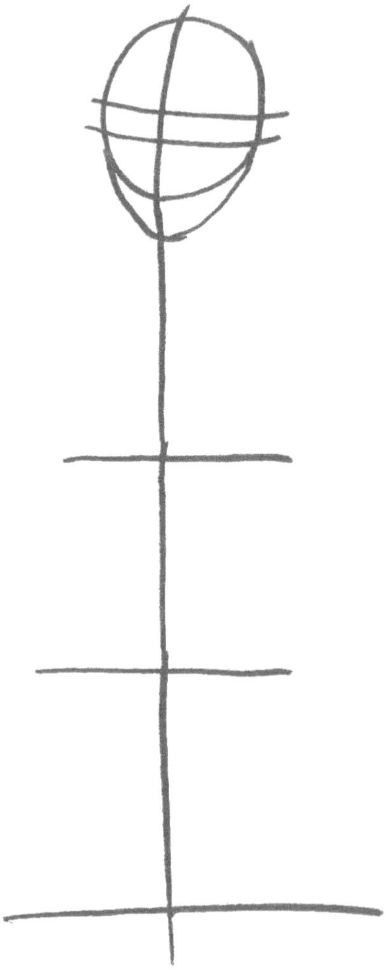

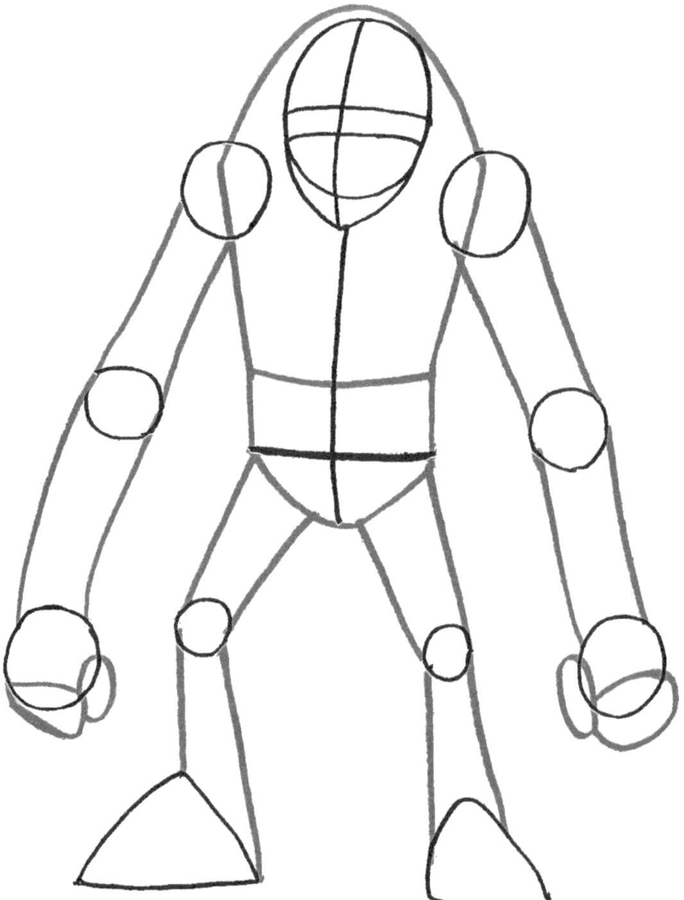

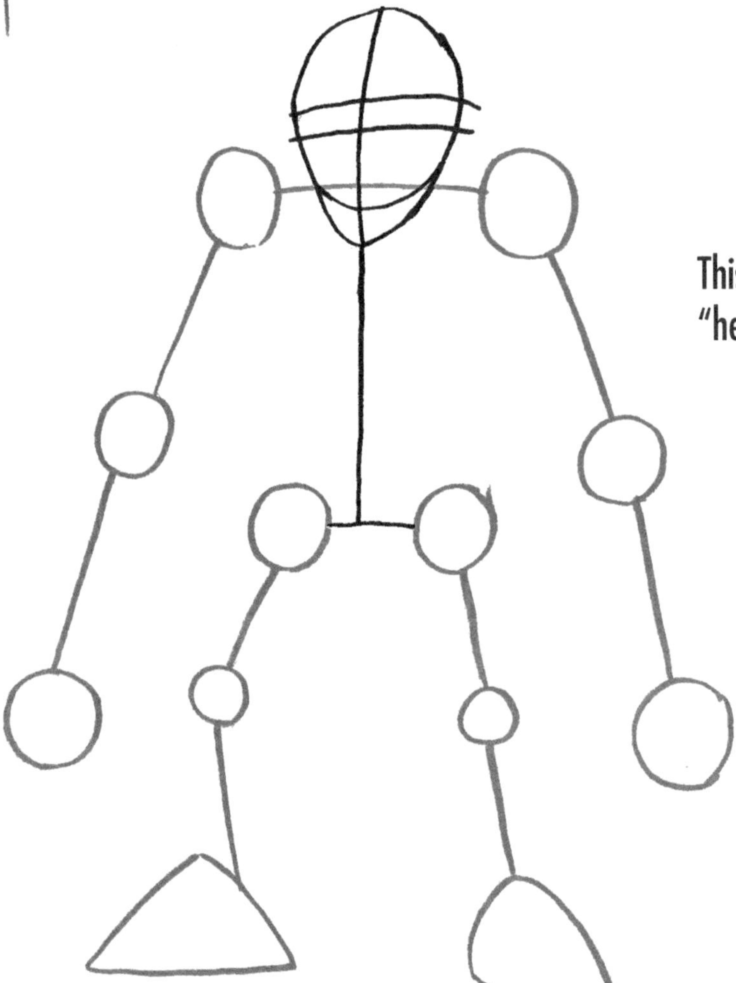

This character is four "heads" tall.

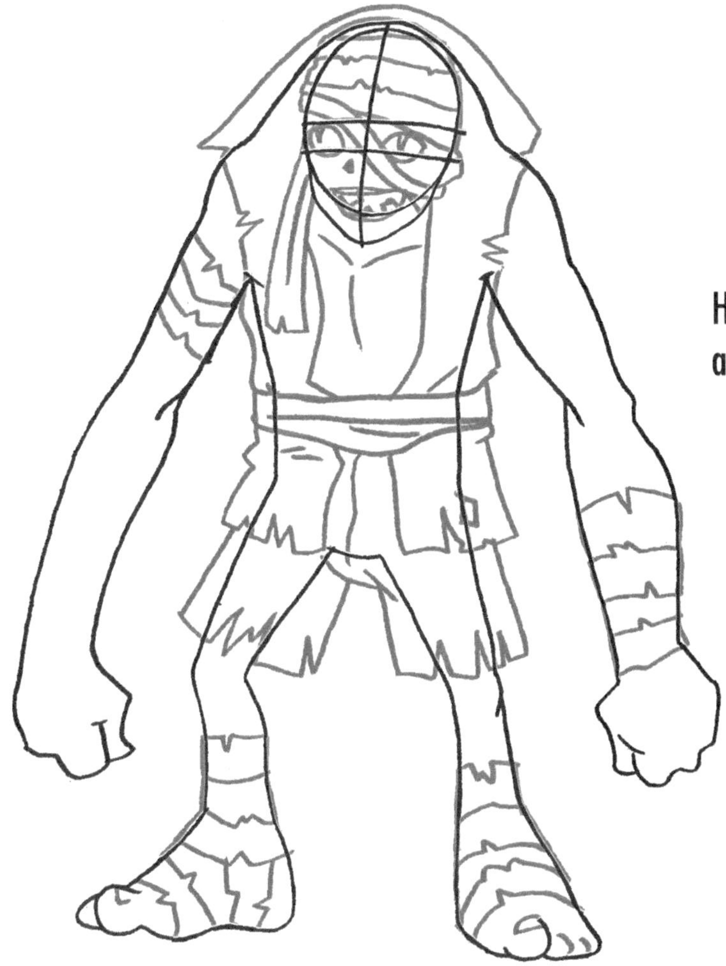

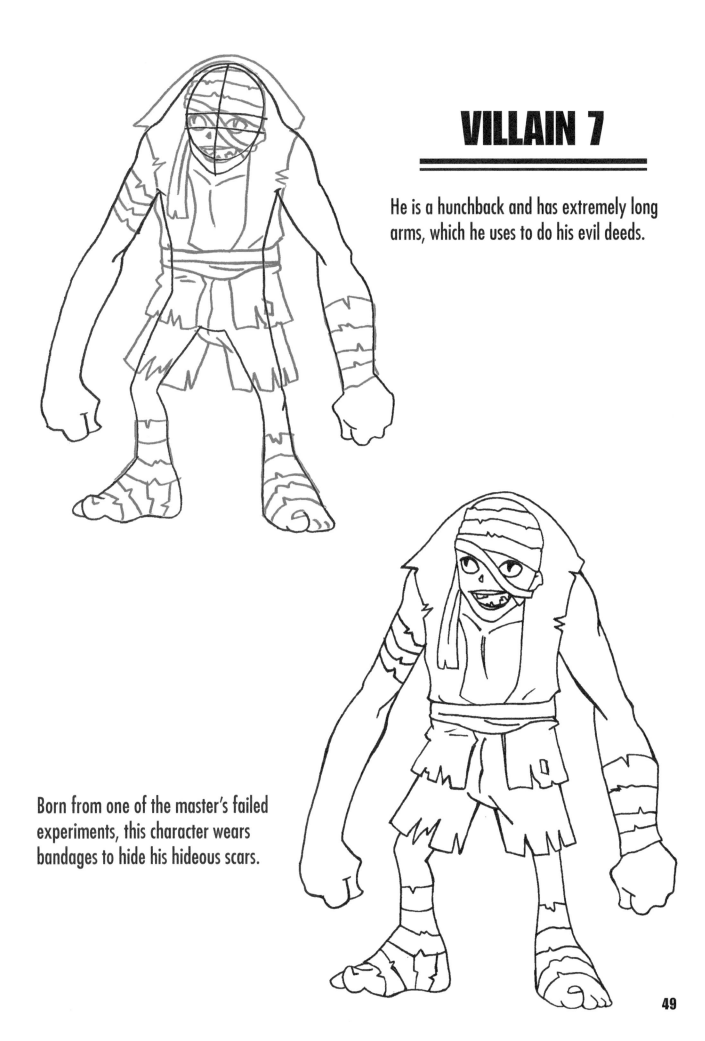

VILLAIN 7

He is a hunchback and has extremely long arms, which he uses to do his evil deeds.

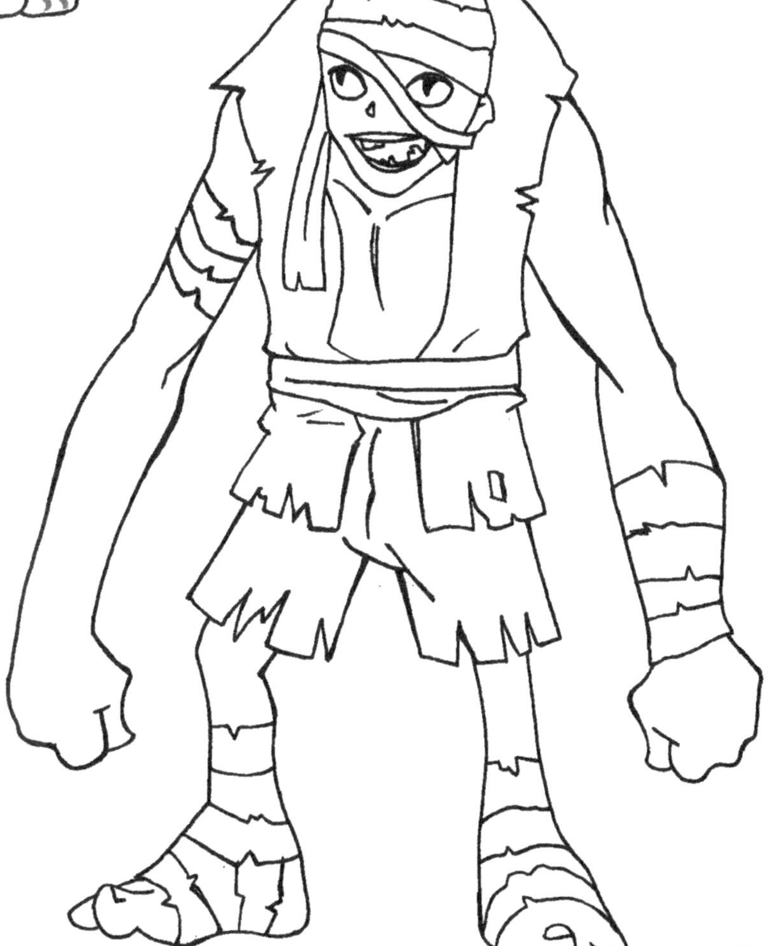

Born from one of the master's failed experiments, this character wears bandages to hide his hideous scars.

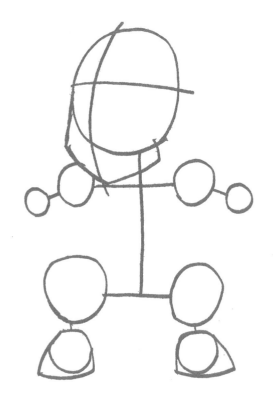

VILLAIN 8

This character is three "heads" tall.

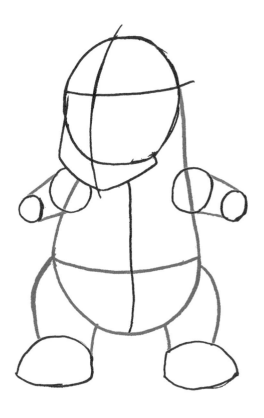

A small monster, he is the master's mascot. His main goal: to ruin the art-school mascot's fun!

CHAPTER 4
The Tournament

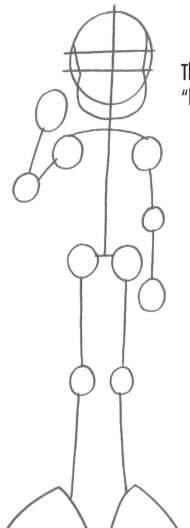

This character is five "heads" tall.

THE REFEREE

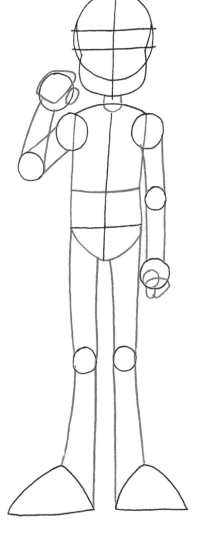

He is the referee of the drawing tournament. He will be the judge when the heroes and villains compete in the drawing contest.

Create Your Own Characters

You can create various characters by using different types of heads. Each will give the character a specific personality.

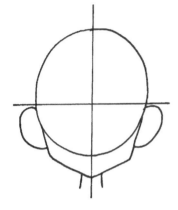

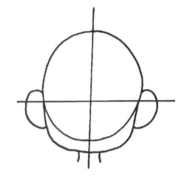

Skull Proportions

You can create different jaw lines from the same basic circle.

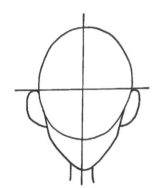

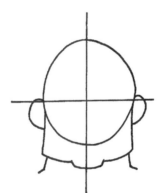

Hairstyles

The character's hairstyle should reflect his or her personality as well.

Eyes

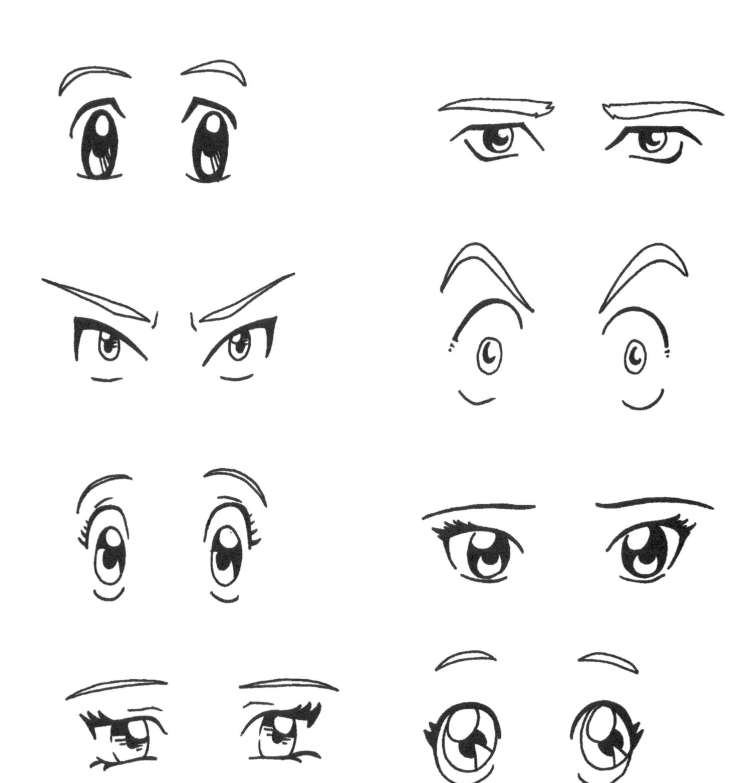

Noses

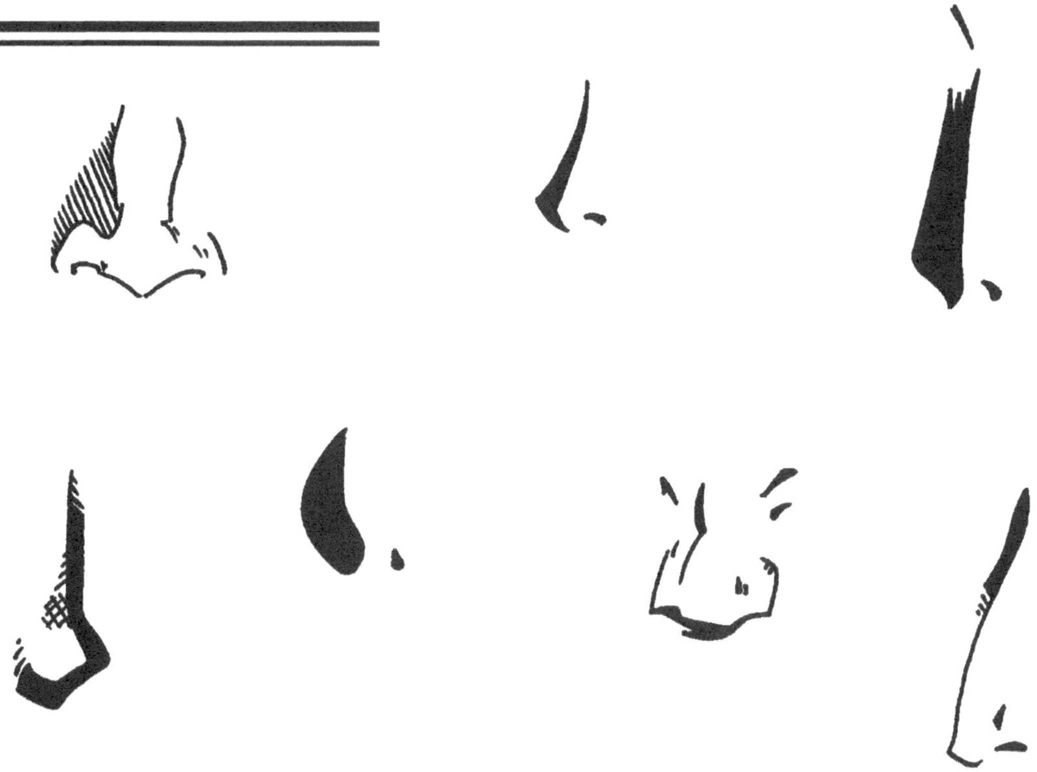

Mouths

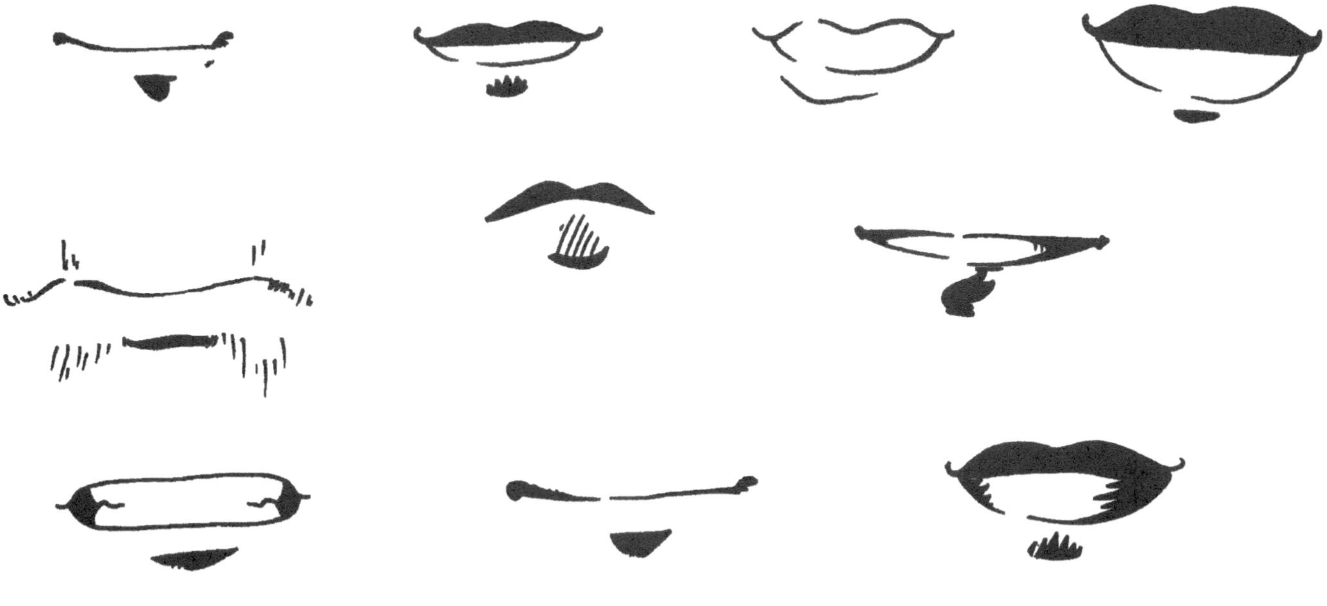

Creating a Story

Every good story has an introduction, a main body, and an ending.

In the introduction, you meet the characters, finding out who they are, where they live, and what they do, for example.

In the main body, you discover the conflict of the story—a problem that the main character, or characters, must overcome.

In the ending, you learn how the main character finally solves the problem.

You are my best student!

Introduction

Our main character studies at the art school.

One day he meets and falls in love with a new student.

Here we meet the characters and learn who they are and what they do.

help!

Main Body

One of the evil master's villains appears.

He kidnaps the new girl. . . .

The villain leaves a ransom note.

"To free the girl, you must enter the drawing tournament!"

Ending

Our main character, the hero, enters the drawing tournament.

He competes against a fierce rival. . . .

"I forgot to practice."

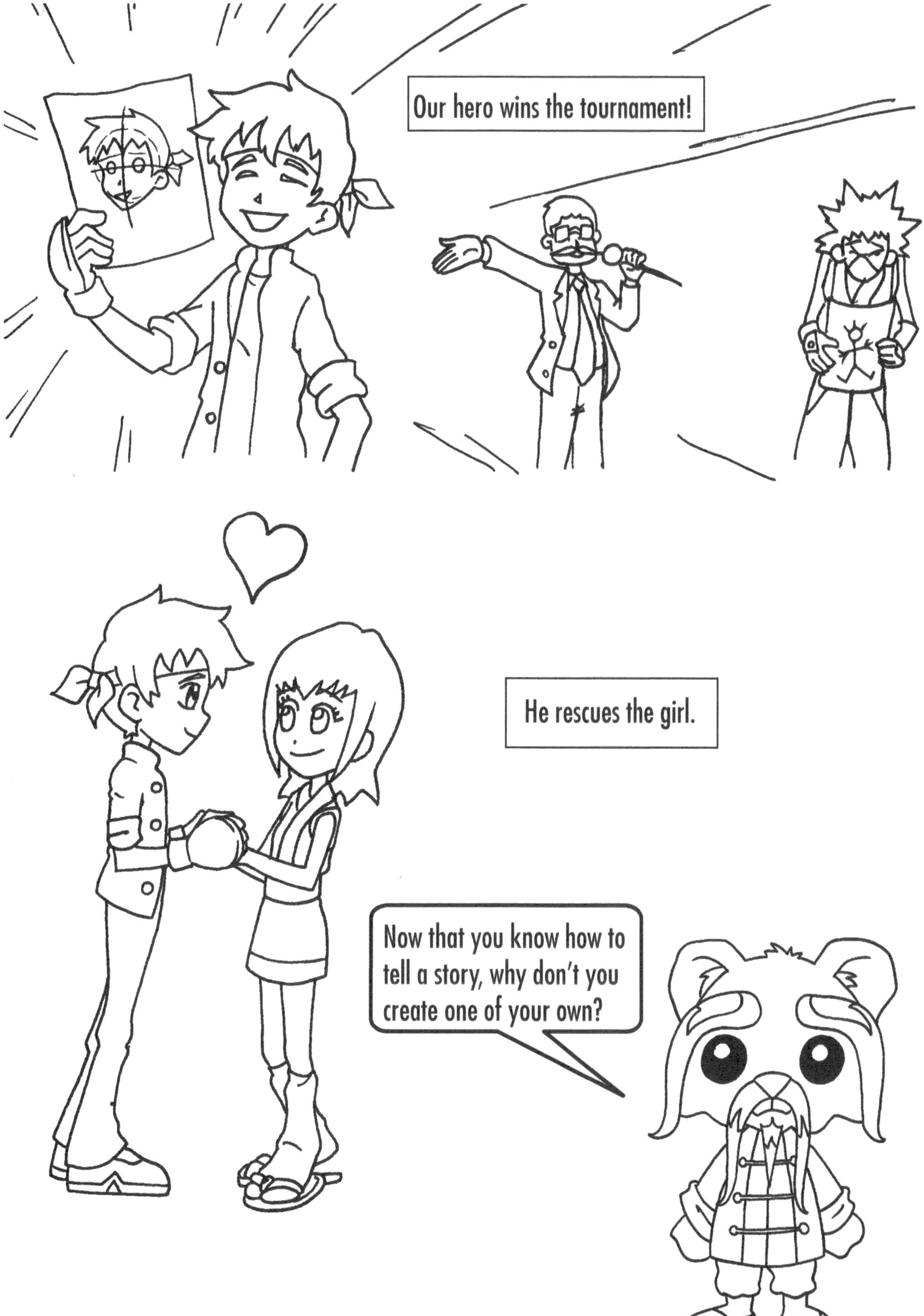
Our hero wins the tournament!
He rescues the girl.
Now that you know how to tell a story, why don't you create one of your own?

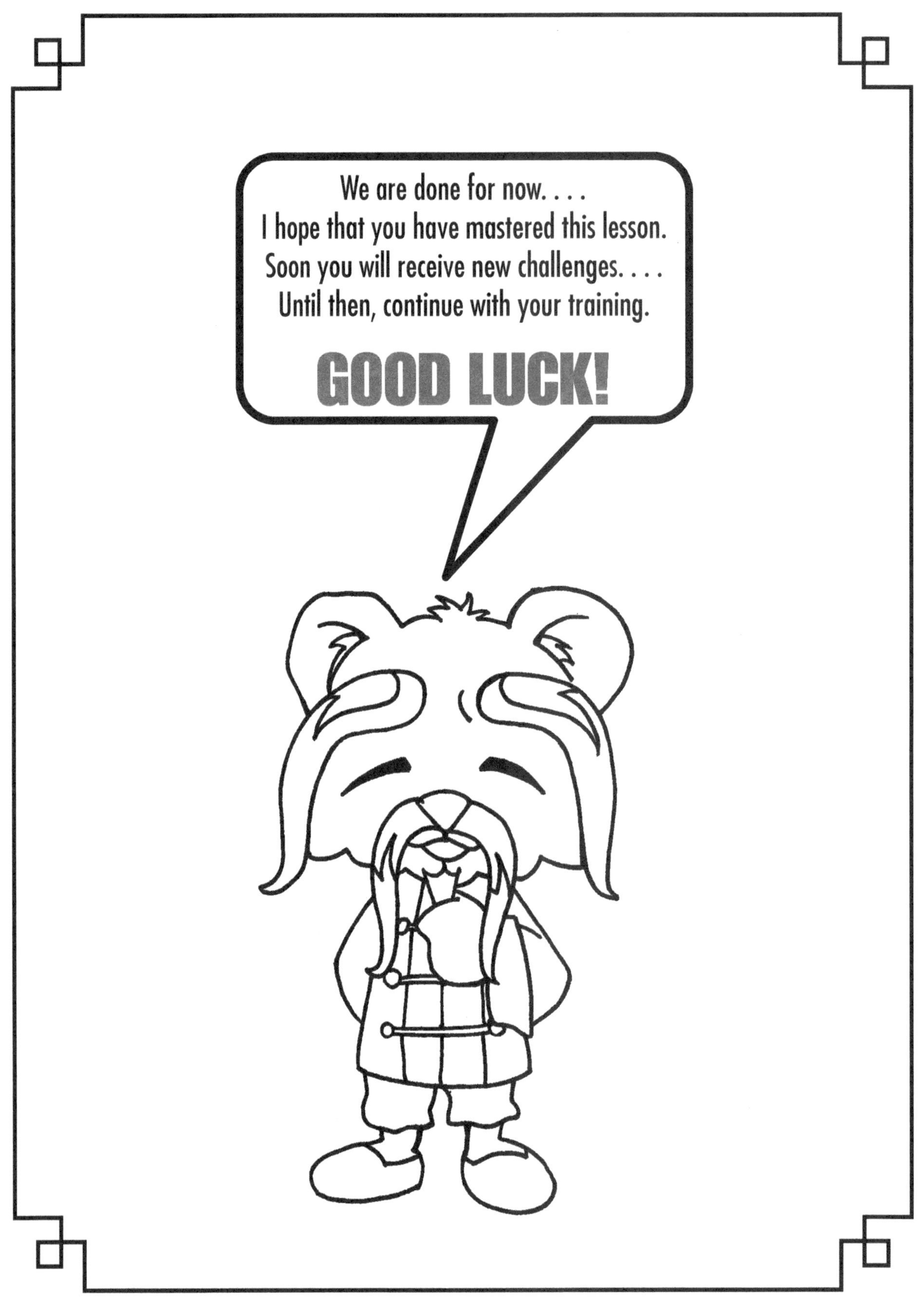
We are done for now. . . .
I hope that you have mastered this lesson.
Soon you will receive new challenges. . . .
Until then, continue with your training.
GOOD LUCK!